The Taxobook

Applications, Implementation, and Integration in Search

Part 3 of a 3-Part Series

Synthesis Lectures on Information Concepts, Retrieval, and Services

Editor

Gary Marchionini, *University of North Carolina, Chapel Hill*

Synthesis Lectures on Information Concepts, Retrieval, and Services is edited by Gary Marchionini of the University of North Carolina. The series will publish 50- to 100-page publications on topics pertaining to information science and applications of technology to information discovery, production, distribution, and management. The scope will largely follow the purview of premier information and computer science conferences, such as ASIST, ACM SIGIR, ACM/IEEE JCDL, and ACM CIKM. Potential topics include, but not are limited to: data models, indexing theory and algorithms, classification, information architecture, information economics, privacy and identity, scholarly communication, bibliometrics and webometrics, personal information management, human information behavior, digital libraries, archives and preservation, cultural informatics, information retrieval evaluation, data fusion, relevance feedback, recommendation systems, question answering, natural language processing for retrieval, text summarization, multimedia retrieval, multilingual retrieval, and exploratory search.

The Taxobook: Applications, Implementation, and Integration in Search: Part 3
Marjorie M.K. Hlava
October 2014

The Taxobook: Principles and Practices of Building Taxonomies: Part 2
Marjorie M.K. Hlava
October 2014

The Taxobook: History, Theories, and Concepts of Knowledge Organization: Part 1
Marjorie M.K. Hlava
October 2014

Children's Internet Search: Using Roles to Understand Children's Search Behavior
Elizabeth Foss and Allison Druin
September 2014

Automated Metadata in Multimedia Information Systems: Creation, Refinement, Use in Surrogates, and Evaluation

Michael G. Christel

2009

The Taxobook: Applications, Implementation, and Integration in Search
Part 3 of a 3-Part Series
Marjorie M.K. Hlava

ISBN: 978-3-031-01162-7   print
ISBN: 978-3-031-02290-6   ebook

DOI 10.1007/978-3-031-02290-6

A Publication in the Morgan & Claypool Publishers series
SYNTHESIS LECTURES ON INFORMATION CONCEPTS, RETRIEVAL, AND SERVICES #37

Series Editor: Gary Marchionini, University of North Carolina, Chapel Hill

Series ISSN 1947-945X Print   1947-9468 Electronic

ABSTRACT

This book is the third of a three-part series on taxonomies, and covers putting your taxonomy into use in as many ways as possible to maximize retrieval for your users. Chapter 1 suggests several items to research and consider before you start your implementation and integration process. It explores the different pieces of software that you will need for your system and what features to look for in each.

Chapter 2 launches with a discussion of how taxonomy terms can be used within a workflow, connecting two—or more—taxonomies, and intelligent coordination of platforms and taxonomies. Microsoft SharePoint is a widely used and popular program, and I consider their use of taxonomies in this chapter. Following that is a discussion of taxonomies and semantic integration and then the relationship between indexing and the hierarchy of a taxonomy.

Chapter 3 ("How is a Taxonomy Connected to Search?") provides discussions and examples of putting taxonomies into use in practical applications. It discusses displaying content based on search, how taxonomy is connected to search, using a taxonomy to guide a searcher, tools for search, including search engines, crawlers and spiders, and search software, the parts of a search-capable system, and then how to assemble that search-capable system. This chapter also examines how to measure quality in search, the different kinds of search, and theories on search from several famous theoreticians—two from the 18th and 19th centuries, and two contemporary. Following that is a section on inverted files, parsing, discovery, and clustering. While you probably don't need a comprehensive understanding of these concepts to build a solid, workable system, enough information is provided for the reader to see how they fit into the overall scheme. This chapter concludes with a look at faceted search and some possibilities for search interfaces.

Chapter 4, "Implementing a Taxonomy in a Database or on a Website," starts where many content systems really should—with the authors, or at least the people who create the content. This chapter discusses matching up various groups of related data to form connections, data visualization and text analytics, and mobile and e-commerce applications for taxonomies. Finally, Chapter 5 presents some educated guesses about the future of knowledge organization.

KEYWORDS

taxonomy, thesaurus, controlled vocabulary, search, retrieval, ontology, knowledge organization, classification, theory of knowledge, metadata

The Taxobook

Applications, Implementation, and Integration in Search

Part 3 of a 3-Part Series

Marjorie M.K. Hlava
Access Innovations, Inc., Albuquerque, New Mexico

SYNTHESIS LECTURES ON INFORMATION CONCEPTS, RETRIEVAL, AND SERVICES #37

Contents

This book is dedicated to all taxonomists, past, present, and future. My team at Access Innovations worked hard and long to bring this book to fruition. It would not have been done without their encouragement, patience, and support.

List of Figures

Preface

Most of us are keenly—personally—aware that over the past several years, information on the Internet has been rapidly expanding, with a flood of information pouring out of computer screens to people everywhere. In 1998, Google reported 3.6 million searches for the year. In 2012, they reported an average of over five billion searches *every* day. That's an increase of over 52 million percent! They claim 67% of the search market, so there remains another 33% of the market of searches to add to that five billion.

We use search often. We use search so often that "Google" has become a verb, at least in practice. "Google it" has become an everyday phrase. Early in my career, searching the Internet (or its precursor, DARPAnet) was the purview of professionals with special training, special access, and special equipment. We were an elite group of gatekeepers, in a way, with access to a corpus of knowledge desirable to researchers but inaccessible except through professional searchers.

In response to our search queries—when we "just Google" something—the search engines like Google, Yahoo, Ask, and others return millions of hits within milliseconds, but how many of those millions of hits does the searcher actually need… or want? How often do you find that the site you seek is at the top of the search results page? How often do you find that the search results don't include what you seek, or that it is buried 10 pages down? How often do you look through 10 pages of search results to see if your desired site is listed at all? How do we contend with this exploding flood of information and find what we actually need? Search needs help!

A parallel expansion—or explosion—has been occurring in intranets, where individual organizational and enterprise information resides. Organizations are eagerly adopting technologies that can locate and sort out the information that is wanted and needed. In this environment, as Jean Graef of the Montague Institute put it shortly after the turn of the millennium, "Taxonomies have recently emerged from the quiet backwaters of biology, book indexing, and library science into the corporate limelight." Corporate librarians, information technology specialists, and others involved in information storage and retrieval recognize and acknowledge the value of taxonomies. However, these people often lack an understanding of taxonomies and of how they are created, maintained, and implemented.

In response, I have developed this guide to taxonomy creation, development, maintenance, and implementation. It will progress rapidly from theory to practice because both are critical for a comprehensive knowledge. The guide is intended to cover the full spectrum from the original scoping of the work through its use in tagging (indexing with keywords from the taxonomy), website navigation, search, author and affiliation/organization disambiguation, identification of peer reviewers, recommendation systems, data mashups, and a myriad of other applications.

In Book 1 (*The Taxobook: History, Theories, and Concepts of Knowledge Organization*) of this three-part series, I introduce the very foundations of classification, starting with the ancient Greek philosophers Plato and Aristotle, as well as Theophrastus and the Roman Pliny the Elder. They were first in a line of distinguished philosophers and thinkers to ponder the organization of the world around them and attempt to apply a structure to that world. I continue by discussing the works and theories of several other philosophers from medieval and Renaissance times, all the way through to notable modern library science figures, including Saints Aquinas and Augustine, William of Occam, Andrea Cesalpino, Carl Linnaeus, René Descartes, John Locke, Immanuel Kant, James Frederick Ferrier, Charles Ammi Cutter, and Melvil Dewey. Part 8 covers the contributions of Shiyali Ramamrita Ranganathan, who is considered by many to be the "father of modern library science." He created the concept of faceted vocabularies, which are widely used—even if they are not well understood—on many e-commerce websites.

I believe that it is important to understand the history of knowledge organization and the differing viewpoints of various philosophers—even if that understanding is only that the differing viewpoints simply exist. Knowing the differing viewpoints will help answer one fundamental question: why do we want to build taxonomies?

With that understanding, the process will go much faster. Taxonomists must think in a different way from the normal subject matter expert way of thinking. Taxonomy thinking is thinking in interconnected outlines. It is not the strictly linear thinking shown in a single taxonomy or hierarchical view of a taxonomy—that list with its increasing levels of specificity– but rather thinking for many people taking many approaches to a subject. Those who can sit in an ivory tower and pursue a single thread of thought to eventually developing a full outline of knowledge from their point of view will only serve their single point of view. They will have converts to their way of thinking, but they will not support an interconnected search world with each individual looking in from their own unique perspective. But you know how that works from the first two volumes, so let's really get to the hands-on work.

In Book 2 (*The Taxobook: Principles and Practices of Building Taxonomies*), I suggest reasons for creating a taxonomy and how it can be used to advantage in an organization. I present and describe various forms of controlled vocabularies, including taxonomies, thesauri, and ontologies, and include methods for constructing taxonomies and other kinds of controlled vocabularies. Standards, especially information standards, are near and dear to my heart, and I have served on several committees and review boards for many of the information standards published by NISO and other standards-forming organizations. Therefore, the last chapter of Book 2 provides an abbreviated list of the specific standards that I feel are most important to knowledge and information professionals, brief descriptions of some of the standards-forming organizations, and the process that they go through in creating these standards or guidelines. While standards might sound like a dry subject best used to cure insomnia, I suggest that they will provide you with an excellent framework for your taxonomy construction project.

Book 3 (*The Taxobook: Applications, Implementations, and Integration in Search*), then, covers putting your taxonomy into use. It's all well and good to create a beautiful taxonomy that classifies The World As We Know It, that conforms to all of the appropriate standards, and is practically perfect in every way, but what good does it do? In order to get back your investment, you have to integrate your taxonomy into whatever workflow or system your organization employs. In Book 3 we discuss the various ways in which you can apply, implement, and integrate your taxonomy into that workflow, with an emphasis on integrating a taxonomy into search. Lastly, I ponder the future of knowledge management. I don't know exactly where we are going, but I have some good guesses based on where we have been and the trends I see in requests from my clients. Based on my guesses, I provide a few suggestions about areas in which you might start to prepare.

While I can't truly predict the future, I am quite certain that the volume of information coming at us isn't going to go away, lessen in intensity, or slow down. The information explosion is going to continue, and we all need to find ways to make sense of it—to improve retrieval, to refine analysis, to pull out the real value of information so that the people who need it, get it.

I hope that you will find this series practical and useful, and perhaps these volumes will become part of your desktop reference collection. Throughout this series, I attempt to include information that will help you to make a business case for your taxonomy construction project, as well as simple-to-use, step-by-step instructions for creating a taxonomy and leveraging it in multiple ways throughout your organization.

Acknowledgments

The series started as a series of talks and lectures given to various groups as full-day workshops on how to build and implement thesauri, controlled vocabularies and databases. The audiences helped hone to message and poked holes in my assertions when appropriate. This was combined with over 600 engagements over the years with fascinating clients who each needed a similar endpoint but with a unique twist because of their content and their individual visions. These combined with the need to educate staff members in how the work is done and creation of best practices as well as broad support on the standards bodies to create an unusual perspective on the knowledge organization and distribution process.

This work would not be possible without the tireless efforts and uncompromising support of many, many, people. My business partner and friend for most of my professional life, Jay Ven Eman has been unstinting in his support and encouragement, although he does occasionally roll his eyes at some of my ideas. The team at Access Innovations, all of whom reviewed the drafts and, in particular, Heather Kotula, Barbara Gilles, Tim Soholt, David (Win) Hansen who massaged the draft, untangled my prose, improved the images and examples and offered very pertinent suggestions to create the final product. Our customers for providing the content and allowing us to work with it have provided an unpararrelled laboratory of material for organization to meet their individual needs. To my own family for their cheerful understanding and putting up with the demands of career and writing, my husband Paul Hlava, my daughters Heather and Holly and their families. And to my mom, Mary Kimmel who showed me that you can have a career and a happy family too.

Many people encouraged me to write down what I was teaching and I am grateful for their continued insistence. Tim Lamkins for his early review and insightful comments, Clients whose works we reference in case studies and examples, and my industry mentors including Roger Summit, Eugene Garfield, Buzzy Basch, Tom Hogan, and Kate Noerr.

To all of these and more I thank you; I could not have done this without you!
Marjorie M.K. Hlava

CHAPTER 1

On Your Mark, Get Ready .... WAIT! Things to Know Before You Start the Implementation Step

You may have already read Books 1 and 2 of this series, which provide the theoretical underpinnings for the implementation of taxonomies, ontologies, and thesauri. Understanding those basics allows a broader perspective in the application of the terms to the content and then to discovery and distribution avenues for that content. The rich content base supports search as well as building of new collections, reaching new communities, and bringing together the researchers who wrote that content, in new and interesting ways.

1.1 DETERMINE YOUR NEEDS

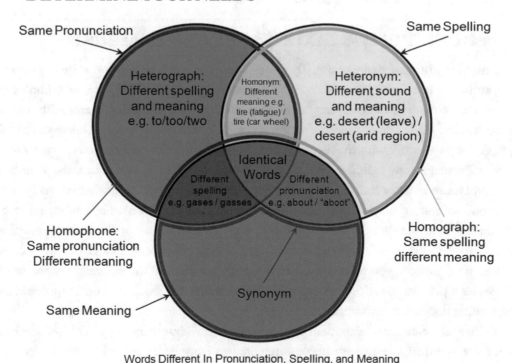

Figure 1.1: Venn diagram with homographs and homophones.

The first order of business when you are building a new thesaurus is to define the scope of the thesaurus—what is in and what is out. These are the subject fields covered and they form the basic thesaurus characteristics. This forms the road map for the production of the entire thesaurus—your semantic system. We covered that in Book 2, Chapter 2 ("Taxonomy Basics") .

Next is to decide what elements each term record should have to modify and extend the options and applications of the thesaurus. There are some basic elements that every term record should have, including the term, broader terms, narrower terms, and related terms. Other elements that you might find useful are scope notes, editorial notes, history, and other elements to track the evolution of terms. We covered this in Book 2, Chapter 4 ("Terms: The Building Blocks of a Taxonomy").

If you expect to have terms that contain diacritical marks, or (from a geocentric viewpoint) "special characters," you will definitely want software that supports Unicode characters or at least a very long list of extended ASCII characters to support other languages and formulas and other notation in mathematics, chemistry, and physics.

If a team, rather than just one person, will be working on the vocabulary or vocabularies, you will want "enterprise" software that will make this feasible, rather than a single user version. When building a taxonomy or ontology, you want that model to be available across the enterprise and not tied to one single person or computer. We'll cover this below.

1.2   SOFTWARE FOR TAXONOMIES AND THESAURI

Taxonomies are not used in a vacuum. They may be part of a full production system, peer review system, author or people net, or a web content management system (CMS) or search implementation. They are certainly used at all parts of the production process to tag documents with controlled vocabulary. Most CMSs do not include a robust tagging or taxonomy system. Unless you are planning to develop and work with the very simplest and smallest of taxonomies, you are going to need software to manage your building process. For creating, developing, expanding, and maintaining one or more taxonomies or thesauri, or for larger vocabularies, you will need what is usually referred to as taxonomy editing or taxonomy creation and maintenance software. For automated or computer-assisted indexing that draws on the information in a taxonomy or thesaurus, you will need indexing (or "categorization") software that integrates with your vocabulary. If you are indexing a collection of documents, you will need a database system, document management system, or CMS that provides a place or "field" for the applied indexing terms, and a way to connect that field to the corresponding documents or webpages.

With many content management system vendors providing some version of taxonomy functionality, users, unfortunately, have become tempted to consolidate and eliminate a very worthy part of their document management process. There are many reasons why a coordinating taxonomy management tool is not only valuable, but necessary. Often, the taxonomy function in CMS systems is limited in several ways. The elements that you want or need for your term records may not be available. Display options may be limited to only a few formats, or even just one format. Updates and additions to the taxonomy may be cumbersome, or in some cases not possible without an added taxonomy management system.

A good taxonomy, based on full term records, will easily work with all the flavors of taxonomy implementation embedded in the content, document, digital asset, database, and other management systems. To manage the taxonomy within one of these systems is to severely limit the options, the applications, and thus the usefulness of the taxonomy to the organization. The purview of the display options for the taxonomy usually rests with the user interface (UI) design team. However, the taxonomy team should provide as much support and direction as possible to ensure that the taxonomy is leveraged well on the UI.

When considering using a content management system's taxonomy feature, you should ask some critical questions, like "Does it just manage the taxonomy—or does it also provide automated classification of any content, in any format and any language?" If tagging is left to the manual process, many users will either not do it at all or tag at a minimum by using top-level terms only. This can only result in horrible search results in the end. If the software tool provides statistical classification, it becomes even more uncontrollable. Although a CMS might be advertised as being capable of handling taxonomies, in reality it might allow only a single broader term in the hierarchy, replicating the library classification systems of old and often not having any cross-hierarchy associations (related term) options. Finally, you will want to know if the CMS under consideration allows synonyms, and then be certain that it allows more than a single synonym for each term.

1.3   TAXONOMY EDITING SOFTWARE

I will always argue for a system for managing taxonomies and business rules to interpret content and apply taxonomy terms that is:

- easily integrated with other systems using application programming interfaces (APIs) and web service calls;

- transparent and human-understandable;

- available to support users as they upload and tag their own content; and

- supportive of searchers by extending to them the full semantic richness of the taxonomy.

The system should not be short-circuited by the limitations of a content management system that, trying to serve an array of purposes, doesn't quite match all the functions served by the original parts.

While terms are the stuff of thesauri, for taxonomies, hierarchies are the glue. Your taxonomy editing software must be able to appropriately handle term hierarchies. This means that it needs to enable you to create—and modify as needed—broader term–narrower term relationships. It needs to automatically work both ways. If you designate Term B as a narrower term of Term A, the software should also automatically establish Term A as a broader term of Term B. It should make the relationship completely visible to the software user as well.

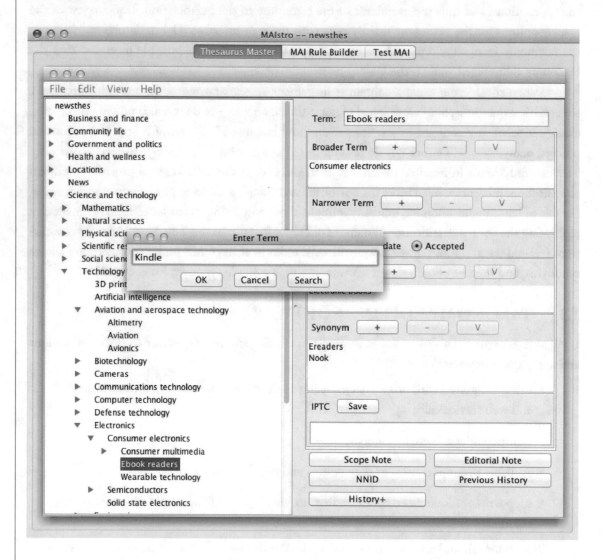

Figure 1.2: Entering a non-preferred term.

For thesauri, the software should enable you to add non-preferred synonyms, and those non-preferred "terms" should be readily visible in the term record display. Searches on the non-preferred terms should provide the "USE" term (the "preferred term") as a result.

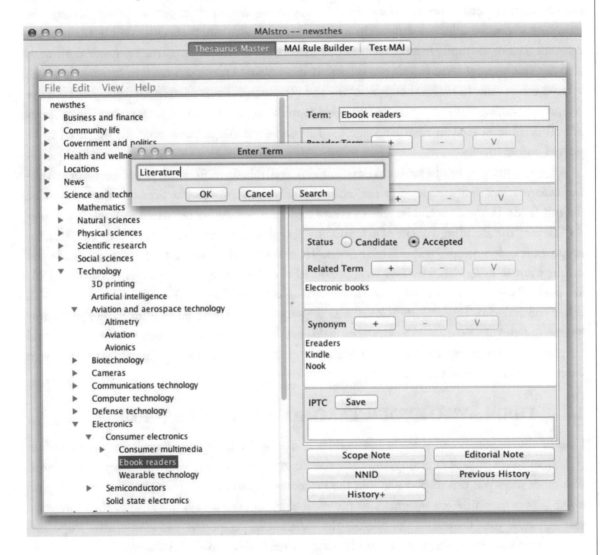

Figure 1.3: Adding a related term.

In the individual term records, the software should allow you to indicate other terms that are already in the thesaurus as related terms. When you establish this associative relationship, it should automatically be reciprocal. That is, while you are working in Term ABC's term record, you might indicate Term XYZ as a term related to Term ABC. Then, you should be able to go to Term XYZ's term record and see in that record that Term ABC has been automatically established as a related term of Term ABC. This reciprocity is important for the overall function of good taxonomy software.

"Postings" is a word used to describe adding a term or term phrase to a list. In choosing the software for taxonomy creations ensure that you are able to check for reciprocal postings: be sure that if you list a term relationship in one place, it is also automatically listed in the position referred to. For example, if a broader term is listed for a narrower term, the narrower term must also list the broader term in its term record. If it is a related term, you want to be sure that both related terms refer to each other. Synonyms and other equivalence relationships also need to have reciprocal postings. This can also be expanded to multilingual thesauri, ensuring that the concepts are all accommodated in each language used in the work. All of these relationships need to be posted automatically.

The software should have a variety of fields available for different types of notes and tracking information that are viewable and editable from the term records. Some of these might be default fields, but you should be able to create custom fields. As we discussed in Book 2, Chapter 4 ("Terms: The Building Blocks of a Taxonomy"), typical notes fields in a thesaurus are those for scope notes, definitions, and editorial notes. There may well be other types of notes fields you might want to add, with whatever term record label or field designation you wish. Custom fields are particularly useful for correlating terms with an external classification coding system, or with other vocabularies. This activity is known as *mapping*. For mapping, you'd want to be able to designate the custom field as an equivalence field, and have it function as such. Notes fields would be plain text for reference purposes, which you could choose to have included—or not—in an external web display of the vocabulary.

1.4   DISPLAYS OF YOUR TAXONOMY OR THESAURUS

One of the exciting challenges in taxonomies is display. With the right graphical user interface (GUI) software or programming, you can produce different views of your taxonomy or thesaurus. The more ways you can display and link the taxonomy, the more different views you can give your users, supporting different insights into the vocabulary and the data it has tagged. The more ways you can view your thesaurus, the broader the variation in perspective you gain on the scope and structure of your vocabulary and the underlying content. Some possibilities are:

- a full hierarchical display (or a multiple level list);

- a systematic listing by term record;

- a strictly alphabetic list;

- a hierarchical list—not necessarily including all the hierarchical levels (although it could), but including a specified number of levels; and,

• mashup displays (mashup displays are discussed later, in Chapter 4, Section 4.3).

1.4.1 PRODUCING THESAURUS VIEWS

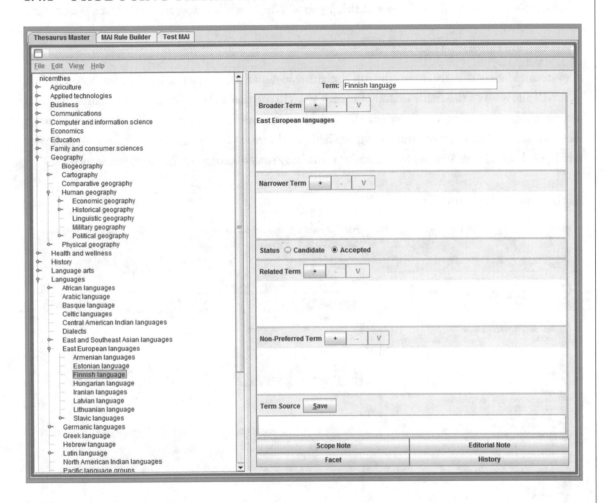

Figure 1.4: Hierarchical view of a taxonomy.

We need to look at alphabetic things—the frequency sorts—several times so we know how many times terms occur in the thesaurus. If there are too many, we should undertake some disambiguation activities. When we have an alphabetic view of our thesaurus, we can begin to look at it using some graphical techniques, and we can start thinking about what kind of views we want to give to the users. I encourage you to try using different views while you are in the building process. When you are working within a specific branch of the taxonomy, on a specific term, but you don't know where else that term is in the thesaurus, you can do a search. You've probably used the Search and Find functions within applications, and that brings up one kind of list view. If you can get a permuted (rearranged [1]) list that will show you that term in context, in the full array of it, in a different format, it will give you a new perspective, which could lead to new insights and ideas. Take a look at some of those "views." I think you will find them more useful than just a search view.

1.4.2   SYSTEMATIC VIEWS

A systematic view usually shows the full thesaurus in alphabetic sequence by full term records. That is, it will show all of the fields existing for each term in the thesaurus. Within the thesaurus, we have term records containing narrower terms, related terms, scope notes, and other fields. The systematic view shows the full term records listing available so that you can see all the related terms, narrower terms, and broader terms of any particular term. This is also known as the full term record view.

Alphabetical Thesaurus View

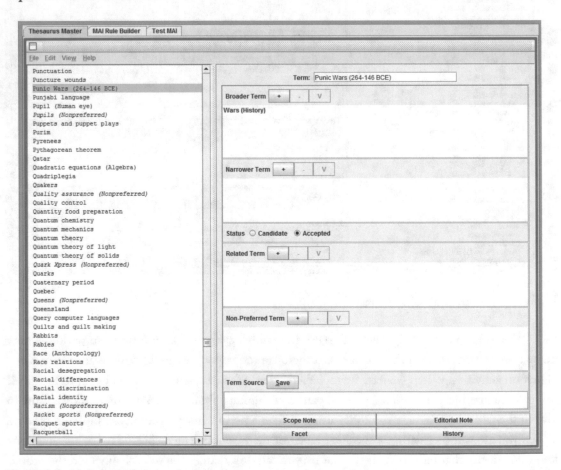

Figure 1.5: Alphabetical view of a taxonomy.

Permuted

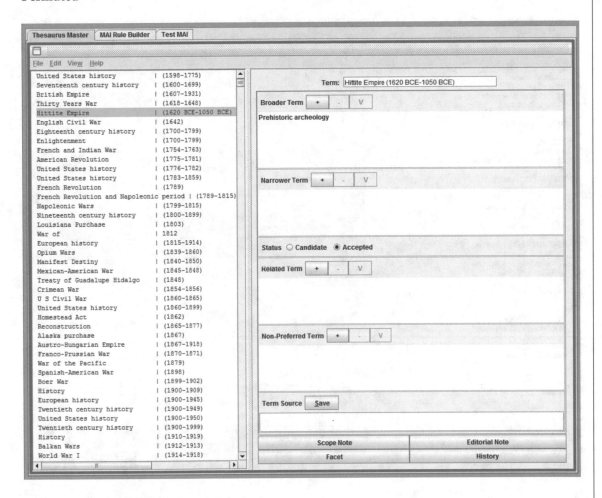

Figure 1.6: Tab permuted view of a taxonomy.

Full term record

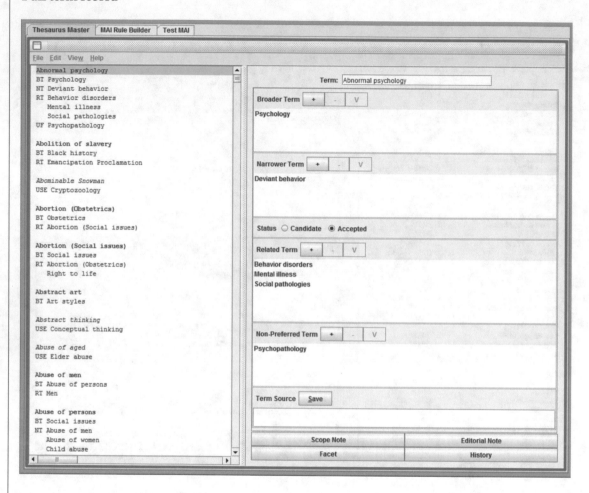

Figure 1.7: View of a term record. The full term record field identifiers are shown in the window on the left.

There are myriad options for viewing your taxonomy. Different software systems will allow you to use different options.

1.5   OUTPUT FORMATS

There are many possible formats for output of the thesaurus record data, and each has its purpose. Here we will discuss three of them—print, web, and automated indexing.

1.5.1   PRINTED OUTPUT

You might output your thesaurus as print—a hard copy book. Normally, if you are going to print, you would do an alphabetic full-term record view as well as a hierarchical view. If you look at a library of printed thesauri, you'll find a myriad of examples. When the Getty Research Institute created their Art and Architecture Thesaurus [2], they hired a thesaurus designer for the several displays in the three-volume printed set.

1.5.2   THESAURUS OUTPUT FOR WEB

If your thesaurus will be available only in digital form, you will still want the basic alphabetic full-term record view and the hierarchical view, but you have many additional options. You may need to create a flat file for implementation on the web or search system, and maybe a structured XML export for a database application to the intended content. You also want to validate the entries and make sure that they have all the necessary pieces of the term record.

Outputting different views and up-posting to multiple broader terms is a frequent request of CMS systems. The system may be predisposed to display only the first three levels of the taxonomy on the web. Currently, it is quite popular to provide the user the data or answer within only three clicks. This means you might want to have a thesaurus display, which is only three levels deep for the web presentation layer. Your thesaurus may have many more levels—be much deeper—and you will use those deeper layers for the actual tagging, but the terms are "rolled up" or "up-posted" to the next higher or broader term until there are only three levels for display. Though we covered this in the structure discussion in Book 2, Chapter 6, I believe it bears repeating here. With "rolling up" or "up-posting," you can index at the most specific level, as the indexing standards recommend, and then display at a much higher level. Combining these two options provides excellent recall and precision while ensuring a fast path to searchers' requests.

1.5.3   THESAURUS OUTPUT FOR AUTOMATED INDEXING

There are many ways to apply the taxonomy to the content. As the size of the collection increases, and the throughput becomes larger, it is increasingly popular to use computer capabilities for indexing automation. These methods vary in degree from an assisted indexing system that suggests terms for editors to choose from, to fully automatic indexing. This is also called automatic categorization, or autocat. Your thesaurus maintenance software may be associated with an automated indexing module. In this case you want to ensure that you have an appropriate import format to support that system. XML [3], SKOS [4], and Zthes [5] are very popular formats for sharing thesauri across systems.

The export format of XML is self-defining and extensible, depending on the needs of the individual thesaurus built. After all, you want your thesaurus to meet the needs of the collection for which it is built. The field elements chosen for a particular thesaurus will vary, and for an ontology they will need to be extended for the relationship extensions as well.

Here is an example of a full term record in XML format.

```
<TermInfo>
 <T>Crystal chemistry</T>
 <BT>Crystals</BT>
 <BT>Physical chemistry</BT>
 <RT>Crystal engineering</RT>
 <RT>Crystalline materials</RT>
 <RT>Crystallography</RT>
 <RT>Supramolecular chemistry</RT>
 <Status>Accepted</Status>
 <History>2006/05/03 11:55 created by Editor1 2006/05/03 11:56 BT
Physical chemistry added by Editor1 2006/05/03 12:47 RT Crystallogra-
phy added by Editor1 2006/05/03 12:48 RT Crystalline materials added
by Editor1 2006/05/03 12:56 RT Supramolecular chemistry added by Ed-
itor1 2006/05/03 13:04 RT Crystal engineering added by Editor1</His-
tory>
 <ttm>crystal chemistry</ttm>
 <CL>801.4, 933.1 (482)</CL>  (Numbers tagged with <CL> refer to Classification Codes.)
 </TermInfo>

<TermInfo>
 <T>Crystal engineering</T>
 <BT>Solid state physics</BT>
 <RT>Crystal chemistry</RT>
 <RT>Crystalline materials</RT>
 <RT>Crystallography</RT>
 <RT>Crystals</RT>
 <RT>Nanostructured materials</RT>
 <RT>Nanotechnology</RT>
 <RT>Supramolecular chemistry</RT>
 <Status>Accepted</Status>
 <History>2006/05/03 13:01 created by Editor1 2006/05/03 13:02 RT
Crystals added by Editor1 2006/05/03 13:03 RT Crystalline materials
added by Editor1 2006/05/03 13:03 RT Nanotechnology added by Edi-
tor1 2006/05/03 13:03 RT Nanostructured materials added by Editor1
2006/05/03 13:04 RT Crystallography added by Editor1 2006/05/03 13:09
RT Supramolecular chemistry added by Editor1 2006/05/03 13:10 BT
Solid state physics added by Editor1</History>
 <ttm>crystal engineering</ttm>
 <CL>933 (482)</CL>
 </TermInfo>
```

There are several advantages to automating the indexing process, and we will cover those in Chapter 2.

1.6   DOCUMENT INDEXING SOFTWARE

Document indexing software should not be confused with book indexing software, which is used in creating back-of-the-book indexes. There are excellent back-of-the-book indexing software systems, but they are not the same as the systems used for document tagging or indexing. Back-of-the-book indexes are pre-coordinate (see the discussion of pre- vs. post-coordinate indexing in Book 2, Chapter 2 ("Taxonomy Basics")). They are not created for use by computers, which use post-coordinate indexes. Keywords are differently formatted than the back-of-the-book term listings. However, there are some document indexing software applications that can be integrated with your taxonomy or thesaurus. Ideally, the software should be able to take advantage of the synonym information in your thesaurus, and to identify the synonyms as triggers for applying the corresponding preferred terms in indexing. Some indexing software enables you to create and modify logical rules for automated indexing, or make indexing suggestions to a human editor. Other indexing software uses pre-programmed algorithms based on statistics.

When you decide that you are going to use a taxonomy or thesaurus, it means that you can build an automatic indexing system faster. Based on the single concept per term approach, the tagger can apply concepts to individual articles or information objects and then build computer algorithms to search those articles. Once a thesaurus is built, it will already have the synonyms, the associated terms, and the broader–narrower term relationships. With that excellent platform in place, it is a straightforward programming task to build a simple rule base automatically. You may then want to modify those rules to achieve high indexing performance. (By *simple rule*, I mean an IF-THEN rule without any complicating conditions.) These are match and identity rules. A *simple* rule (also known as an *identity rule*) might look something like this:

IF *Automobiles*, USE *automobiles*

In a *simple* or *identity rule*, the triggering text is identical to the USE term. In some database and content management systems that treat taxonomy and indexing functions as ancillary, *simple* or *identity rules* are the only option available.

However, in a more robust system, and if you are using a thesaurus, you could have *simple* rules that are *synonym rules*, like this one:

IF *Cars*, USE *Automobiles*

Things can get a little—or a lot—more complex with *complex rules*:

IF *Cars* AND NEAR *Electricity*, USE *Electric Cars*

If you use indexing software that can be integrated with a taxonomy or thesaurus, the software may have a configuration option that lets you specify whether to apply broader terms to resources, along with their more specific narrower terms, or just apply the most specific terms. You will need to decide which option will work best for your particular situation.

The thesaurus determines the depth of the indexing. You can only use the terms that exist in the thesaurus. Therefore, you can only index as deep, or as specifically, as the terms in the thesaurus support. As Aitchison, Gilchrist, and Bawden note, "the fuller and more accessible the thesaurus, the more scope will be offered to the indexer" [6].

To take full advantage of your taxonomy or thesaurus, there are two main considerations when you index:

1. **Depth:** Are you indexing to the full depth of the taxonomy or thesaurus, to the extent applicable in the individual articles?

2. **Breadth:** Are you indexing to the full range of thesaurus concepts appearing in the individual articles?

With these two concepts in mind, you are able to support both precision (depth) and recall (breadth) in search.

1.7   SAVE A PLACE FOR THE METADATA!: DATABASE SYSTEMS AND CONTENT MANAGEMENT SYSTEMS

You built a thesaurus. You tagged your data. **You need a place to put the terms**. That seems to be a frequently overlooked detail. You build the taxonomy; you are applying the taxonomy to the data; you need a field for the taxonomy term—or terms—in each database record. It doesn't matter what you call the field, but in your content management or document management system or database application, you will most certainly need to build in a field to hold those taxonomy terms. Make sure you use the Meta Name="Keyword" field in the HTML header of your webpages.

We see a lot of the Fire-Aim-Ready approach, as in: "I bought and set up the hardware, I chose software package X, and I'm ready to put the data in the software. Well, there's no room for that piece of data, there's no field for indexing terms, so we are not going to put that in our database." There's no room for a taxonomy, and no field for taxonomy terms in your new database, so you can't do it. Well, you just wasted a bunch of time and money!

I suggest you take the Ready-Aim-Fire approach instead. Ready: Look at your data and assess your needs. Aim: Build the taxonomy that fits the data. Then, and only then, Fire!: choose the content management or document management system or database application that will support your data, and then arrange for the hardware to support it all.

```
1  <!DOCTYPE html PUBLIC "-//W3C//DTD XHTML 1.0 Transitional//EN"
   "http://www.w3.org/TR/xhtml1/DTD/xhtml1-transitional.dtd">
2  <html xmlns="http://www.w3.org/1999/xhtml"><head></head><!-- InstanceBegin
   template="/Templates/integrity.dwt" codeOutsideHTMLIsLocked="false" --><head>
3
4  <meta http-equiv="Content-Type" content="text/html; charset=utf-8" />
5  <script type="text/javascript" src="http://peak-ip-54.com/js/21758.js" ></script>
6  <noscript><img src="http://peak-ip-54.com/images/track/21758.png?
   trk_user=21758&trk_tit=jsdisabled&trk_ref=jsdisabled&trk_loc=jsdisabled" height="0px"
   width="0px" style="display:none;" /></noscript>
7  <!-- InstanceBeginEditable name="doctitle" -->
8  <title>Access Integrity Medical Transaction Analysis</title>
9  <!-- InstanceEndEditable -->
10 <!-- InstanceBeginEditable name="head" -->
11 <meta name="keywords" content="Access Integrity, CPTTagger, HCPCSTagger, ICDTagger,
   Medical Claims Compliance, claims analysis, medical billing, medical claims, medical
   coding, medical transactions" />
12 <meta name="description" content="Access Integrity's Medical Claims Compliance
   automatically extracts relevant content from electronic medical records (EMR), procedure
   notes and key patient medical facts and provides an in-depth analysis during the medical
   claims workflow process." />
13 <!-- InstanceEndEditable -->
14 <link rel="shortcut icon" href="favicon.ico" >
15 <link rel="stylesheet" type="text/css" href="/css/main.css" />
16 <link href="/templates/p7exp/p7exp.css" rel="stylesheet" type="text/css" />
17
18 <script type="text/javascript">
19   var _gaq = _gaq || [];
20   _gaq.push(['_setAccount', 'UA-16849414-1']);
21   _gaq.push(['_setDomainName', 'none']);
22   _gaq.push(['_setAllowLinker', true]);
23   _gaq.push(['_trackPageview']);
24
25   (function() {
26     var ga = document.createElement('script'); ga.type = 'text/javascript'; ga.async =
   true;
27     ga.src = ('https:' == document.location.protocol ? 'https://ssl' : 'http://www') +
   '.google-analytics.com/ga.js';
28     var s = document.getElementsByTagName('script')[0]; s.parentNode.insertBefore(ga,
   s);
29   })();
30 </script>
31
32
33 </head>
34
```

Figure 1.8: HTML header source code showing the meta name="keywords" field.

1.8   SEARCH SOFTWARE

There are dozens of search software options available to you, and again, as with taxonomy software and content management or document management system or database application software, a needs assessment process before going down that road is advisable.

Here are just a few of the options you might want to consider.

- An online user interface for searching might have a taxonomy or thesaurus behind the scenes. The interface might suggest an indexing term through auto-completion, based on the first several letters of a search string that the user has entered.

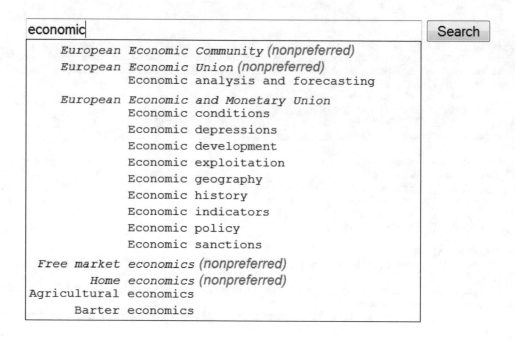

Figure 1.9: Auto-completion function in search at www.mediasleuth.com.

- The interface might also offer possibilities for narrowing or expanding a search, based on a search term's narrower or broader terms.

Economics

Observes that science and technology have led to economic development, and notes that economic forces control the allocation of resources to research. Considers agriculture, the coal industry, magnetic resonance in disease detection, and satellite communications as technologies affected by economic
Descriptors : Medical **economics** - Technology and civilization
http://www.mediasleuth.com/21877-Economics.htm

An Introduction to **Economics**

Presents Professor Viksnin's survey of economic policies over the past decade as the framework within which management and mismanagement of the economy are discussed. Covers such topics as unemployment, inflation, tax return, money supply, balance of payments and international value of the dollar an
Descriptors : **Economics** - History of **economics** - Economists
http://www.mediasleuth.com/8605-An-Introduction-to-Economics.htm

Very Basic **Economics**

Presents a basic **economics** lesson regarding supply and demand, specialization, division of labor
Descriptors : **Economics**
http://www.mediasleuth.com/6841-Very-Basic-Economics.htm

Understanding **Economics**

Introduces students to the subject of **economics**. Focuses on some of the revised national content
Descriptors : **Economics** - Marketing
http://www.mediasleuth.com/54349-Understanding-Economics.htm

Economics with Hobbyda

principles of **economics**. Part of a series on **economics**.
Descriptors : **Economics** - Economic systems - Supply and demand (**Economics**) - Consumption (**Economics**)
http://www.mediasleuth.com/48304-Economics-with-Hobbyda.htm

> **Expand your search**
-*Thesaurus Related Terms*

Economists

> **Target your search**
-*Thesaurus Narrower Terms* Area
economy
Consumption (Economics)
Economic analysis and
forecasting
Economic conditions
Economic development
Economic indicators
Economic policy
Economic sectors
Economic systems
Economic theory
Environmental economics
European Union
Finance
History of economics
Insurance
International economic relations
Waste (Economics)

Figure 1.10: View of www.mediasleuth.com showing "Expand your search" and "Target (narrow) your search" functions.

- The search interface might suggest related topics of possible interest to search on, based on the search term's related terms in the associated thesaurus.

- Alternatively, or additionally, the interface might provide the user with the opportunity to browse and search a taxonomy or thesaurus, to discover and enter keywords with which the desired material is likely to be indexed.

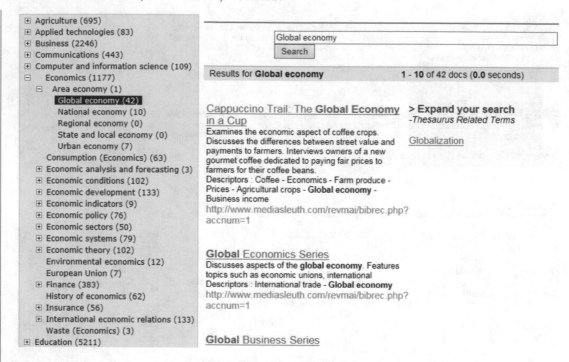

Figure 1.11: Browse view of a taxonomy at www.mediasleuth.com.

These are all good features for a potential search software system. As with choosing your content management or document management system or database application, determine what your data and your users need, and what they want, before you investigate different purchase options.

In addition, when a search software vendor says that the software can fully use a taxonomy, find out what that actually means. Ask the following questions.

- Is the vendor using the word "taxonomy" as explained by W3C, or by ISO and ANSI/NISO? (The latter are more robust.)

- Can the software load synonyms to the search indexes? Is there a limit on how many synonyms you can have, both for the entire taxonomy and for individual terms?

- Can the software use and show the hierarchy in the search results?

- Does the software allow related terms to take the user across hierarchies to other topical areas?

- How are the taxonomy terms added to the data in the collection you are indexing? Manually or automatically? Are they controlled terms or are they automatically generated by statistical pointers (uncontrolled terms)?

If the vendor claims that you can manage the terms from within their system, ask if you can add related terms (associations), broader and narrower terms (hierarchies), multiple broader terms (polyhierarchy), and synonyms (equivalence terms). Where do scope notes go? Does the system keep a history of activities on terms, i.e., an audit trail?

Search is covered in more detail in Chapter 3. I hope you will take the time to study that chapter before making any purchasing decisions.

CHAPTER 2

Taxonomy and Thesaurus Implementation

2.1   HOW TAXONOMY TERMS ARE USED

We have looked at various topics involving taxonomies and thesauri, and we have seen that controlled vocabularies are an important part of search and browsing. But how are taxonomies put to use? What about the terms? Where do they go? Exactly how are they put to use in search? What are the different ways that a taxonomy can be used in search? The boundaries of taxonomy creation and information architecture are overlapping. To start understanding the answers to these questions, let's look at a webpage.

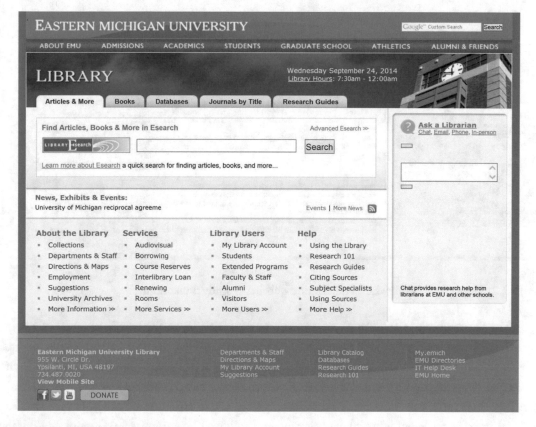

Figure 2.1: The Eastern Michigan University Library home page.

The Google search bar near the top searches the whole site. The tabs below it navigate to different parts of the site. With the Library Esearch button you can find "articles, books, and more." There is a navigation menu near the bottom for browsing by topic. However, do all of those things really provide a complete search? The interface gives the impression that users are searching all kinds of different places, but there is no way of knowing if that's really the case.

Another way of providing website search capabilities is to use a taxonomy or thesaurus to drive searches.

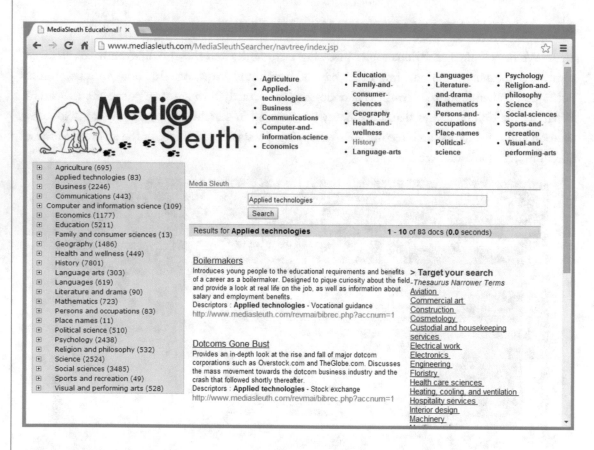

Figure 2.2: Example of using the MediaSleuth website to study a taxonomy.

The figure above is an example of a search presentation layer. The top-level terms of a taxonomy are displayed on the left side as an active webpage that allows the user to explore the hierarchy of terms within the taxonomy. In order to gain firsthand experience with these ideas, you are invited to exercise the webpage at http://www.mediasleuth.com/MediaSleuthSearcher/navtree/index.jsp. Each top-level term can have many terms arranged in a tree structure below it. Notice that each top-level term is preceded a boxed plus sign by and followed by parentheses containing a number.

For example, the second term from the top of the list of top terms " + Applied technologies (83)" has the number 83 in parentheses following it, indicating that 83 items match the top term *Applied technologies*. Clicking on the + sign before the term expands the list of terms below *Applied technologies* to show the 26 thesaurus terms below it.

Near the top of Figure 2.2 there is a search button associated with an input box where you can see auto-completion at work for the selection of search terms from the taxonomy. As characters are typed into the search box, preferred and non-preferred terms from the taxonomy that match the partially typed portion of a word are listed for the user to select. In some implementations, frequent misspellings such as Orthopeadics are included in the list. You don't need to know the entire taxonomy. Searches can be performed on either synonyms or preferred forms. A drop-down list appears as you type, guiding you through the thesaurus. Clicking on a drop-down list element gives search results associated with the selected item for the selected term.

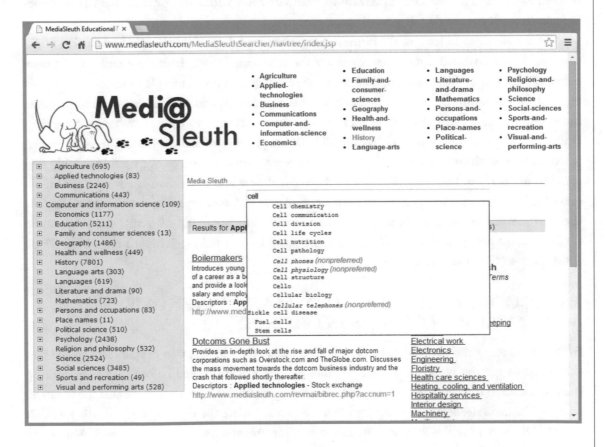

Figure 2.3: Auto-completion function at www.mediasleuth.com showing the drop-down list feature.

When the search comes back, in this case on *Cells*, related terms are displayed that provide suggestions for further search, as do the narrower terms of the term originally searched on. All of that is served up from the taxonomy.

A thesaurus can also be used to generate index terms from a group of information objects such as books or articles that can populate a database management system (DBMS). The DBMS can then serve up information objects containing the concepts captured in the thesaurus.

2.2   CONNECTING TAXONOMIES

I've been asked if taxonomies can be connected. The short answer is "yes." The long answer is "Yes, if…" If the taxonomies are standardized, or at least mostly standardized, it seems that there should be a way that taxonomies can be connected in various organizational systems, and once built, can be used and reused by separate organizations or departments within one organization. Taxonomies are usually built to cover a fairly small range of topics.

First we need to look at the format of the taxonomy data. If it is in XML, what DTD did you use? What standard did you use to create the taxonomy? If you have taxonomies that follow either the ISO or NISO standard, chances are excellent that you will be able to import and export most of the taxonomy automatically. By doing this, you can expand one taxonomy with the other, increasing the detail in key areas, or pull sections from each to create an entirely new taxonomy. If you have three taxonomies and they are all built using the same standards and the same format, it would be straightforward to merge all three of them. After the merge, we would probably find some terms that are not congruent, and a thorough review and evaluation is advisable. Terms in one of the taxonomies merged might have a completely different meaning that is undesirable for the new merged taxonomy. Generally this occurs with only a handful of terms, and they can be disambiguated using modifiers. When this is not possible, we would seek input from SMEs (Book 2, Chapter 6 ("Evaluation and Maintenance")).

2.3   COORDINATING PLATFORM AND TAXONOMY IMPLEMENTATIONS INTELLIGENTLY

Allow me to step onto my soapbox and rant for a moment: Why is it that people seem to feel that they need to get the platform and the technology in place and tested before they ever work on the organization of their information and cleaning up the data? They do not look at the data and what hardware is needed by the user community to manipulate the data. I am repeatedly told that the DTD/schema for the data and the taxonomy implementation have been delayed because the computation platform needs improvement. What is the platform for? Without well-organized and well-formed test data, how can the system be tested? How do they know that the user can find anything in the proposed system if they have no idea what the data is like? Where are the taxonomy terms going to go in the database or the record or the system? How are they bound to the information they reference? Building the platform first is like buying a pair of shoes without knowing either the size of the foot or the occasion for which they are to be worn!

To a certain extent, the performance of a computational system can be predicted when simple aspects of the data are known. For example, the fact that the common crawl data is 81 terabytes broken up into 5 billion webpages, means that if you put that data on one computer with 30 three-terabyte disk drives, it would take 10 days to read the data once. We can also predict that if we put the same data onto 30 computers, each with a 3-terabyte disk drive, then we could read the data in 8 hours. And this is not a vacuous observation because, for most computations on library type data, the input and output times dominate the computation.

How would I rather see the implementation? Using the following five steps for a solid platform implementation.

1. **Users first:** What do they use now? You can discover that from what they check out or view in the current system. What kind of data do they need? What are their null queries (search queries that return no positive results; "Your search did not match any articles" and "Your search has produced no results" are two examples) on the current system? What are they looking for and cannot find? What are they calling their colleagues to help them find since it is not available on their system? Ask them what they would like to have, and cross-check their answers by looking at what they are doing now.

2. **Data second:** What do you have now? What is it like? How is it currently organized? How is it named? What are the data types and formats? How many collections are there? Should they be merged? How clean is the data? By "clean data" we mean data that is well formatted and consistently tagged.

3. **Third, mapping the ideal solution:** I know that the "ideal" is not always achievable, but you cannot even begin to approach "ideal" if you don't know what "ideal" is to start. It doesn't hurt to ask what the ideal user environment would be. What would be the preferred data offering? How do you want to display it, search it, organize it? The taxonomy is important to all three of these factors, so map it out early.

4. **Specify the ideal:** Create the DTD/schema for the ideal data set. An XML schema has two main parts to it: (1) The elements (fields) you want included, and (2) the attribute tables, which tell you how you will fill those elements. How would you organize it?

5. **Lastly, assess the road map to the "ideal":** How flexible should the model be? Is the model extensible? What is the current status? How much of the ideal do you have

now? What do you need to add? Does it exist? Who has it? Would you have to build it or can you buy it? What are the semantic enhancements going to be? How will they be accommodated in the platform? Can the platform handle the taxonomy? How big will it be? How will it be applied? Where do the taxonomy terms get placed, in the system or the data record?

Is getting to the "ideal" situation achievable? It often is! However, I am frequently amazed to find how many people plan to implement a taxonomy but have no way to attach taxonomy terms to an information object, article, or record on the platform. They have no way to search them, no way to display them. "We knew they were important, planned for them the whole time…." Okay—but where do you want them to go?

With the initial schema in place, I would massage the data to match the new XML schema and plan to extend the schema as the data becomes known. The best XML schema in the world will need to be augmented by the real data. Finalizing the schema early, as "the systems guys" often want to do, will cause difficulties later in the process. See what the data is really like, build a schema to codify it, and then build the database platform. Building the platform first will mean that you have to shoehorn the data into something that is not quite the same shape as the data. Data bunions quickly result!

If you plan early to accommodate the data itself, most delays and headaches of the normal platform implementation are avoided. Save yourself a lot of money and heartache! Look at the data and how it is going to be semantically enhanced first. Find out what your users need, what they want, and what they will actually use. Then construct the platform—any other approach is backward.

2.4   RDF: A WRAPPER FOR METADATA

The Resource Description Framework (RDF) has moved into the mainstream with the creation of triples and triple stores from taxonomies, thesauri, and ontologies. RDF provides a means of "wrapping" these metadata items that describe terms in a particular way. (Triples are described in more detail below.) In information management, a *wrapper* [7] is a program that translates tagged data into *relational* form [8], so that databases can deal with it. We're interested in this because some of that tagged data includes taxonomy terms that have been used to describe documents.

One forerunner of present-day wrappers was an attempt by the Internet Engineering Task Force (IETF [9]) to develop standards for World Wide Web resources. They came up with uniform resource characteristics (URCs [10]). IETF defined a URC as a set of meta-level information about a resource. Some examples of such meta-information are owner, encoding, access restrictions (perhaps for particular instances), and cost.

The URCs concisely defined how a Uniform Resource Locator (URL) or a Uniform Resource Name (URN) or a Unique Identifier (UID) or any of those unique items could be uniformly defined so that everybody would do it the same way. The idea was that with a simple batch of metadata you could connect everything. It languished for about 10 years.

As the URCs faded, attention shifted to RDF [11], a wrapper that you could put around something like a bibliographic record or even full text of a full document and transmit it to another computer system. The wrapper would contain the document type definition (DTD) or the SGML declaration, or at least a link to it so all information about how a record was encoded would be included with the record, making it possible to open it on any system. It has become much more involved and much fancier over the years.

Originally, RDF was a self-documenting format, a framework to describe whatever was there. In 1995, when it was developed, RDF was a way of putting a wrapper around information so that you could see and interpret what someone has sent to you. For example, if you sent me an RDF file, you would be sending me a file and also sending me the DTD that went with it so that I could interpret the data. The nice, clean RDF wrapper explained what was in there. It is still a nice framework for doing that. However, it has taken on a different life now.

RDF syntax is pretty straightforward because it follows the XML syntax. XML syntax is commonly used to store instances of described resources and to communicate those instances among applications.

Schemas can be declared in XML to disambiguate semantics among resource description communities. They might also be tied to something like the Dublin Core. The RDF schemas can be used to declare existing vocabularies (e.g., Dublin Core) and used to declare unique vocabularies or sets of metadata required by specific communities. Simply put, it declares a set of resources and their properties and their interrelationships. It forms the current basis for the W3C's Simple Knowledge Organization System (SKOS). SKOS is a family of formal languages designed for representing controlled vocabularies. Because it is related to and strongly linked to Dublin Core but not to the Z39.19 standards, SKOS does not include all the options that are available from the NISO standard. Some are left out of the SKOS declaration, causing loss of some of the relationships within the thesaurus.

An RDF does not have to be Dublin Core; it can be something completely separate. In fact, when W3C came out with SKOS as an export format for taxonomies, they were using that as a formal language to describe the way that taxonomies or vocabularies were exported. Unfortunately, they did not include everything in the first edition that one might need, so you couldn't have multiple broader terms, you couldn't have synonyms, and you couldn't have related terms. It was very limiting! However, you could have a broader or narrower term. It was for classification systems, but not for thesauri. Taxonomies, as we have seen, may include more than just the hierarchy formed by broader and narrower term relationships. The newer editions of SKOS include more options so that you can export null information, which means you can export a full NISO/ISO thesaurus in a SKOS format by including the additional information that SKOS does not use natively in the NULL element.

Here's an RDF wrapper on a set of information so you can see how the format appears:

```
<rdf:RDF
  xmlns:rdf="http://www.w3.org/TR/WD-rdf-syntax#"
  xmlns:dc="http://purl.org/dc/elements/1.0/"
  xmlns:dcq="http://purl.org/dc/qualifiers/1.0/">
  <rdf:Description about="urn:issn:1361-3197">
  <dc:Title>Ariadne</dc:Title>
  <dc:Subject>
    journal; magazine; elib; electronic libraries; digital libraries;
    networking; Web; IT; higher education
  </dc:Subject>
  <dc:Description>
    A print magazine of Internet issues for librarians
    and information specialists
  </dc:Description>
  <dc:Publisher>
    Information Services, University of Abertay, Dundee
  </dc:Publisher>
  <dc:Type>Text.Serial.Magazine</dc:Type>
  <dc:Relation>
    <rdf:Description>
    <dcq:RelationType
      rdf:resource="http://purl.org/dc/vocabularies/AgentTypes/v1.0/Is-
BasisFor"/>
    <rdf:value resource="http://www.ariadne.ac.uk/"/>
    </rdf:Description>
  </dc:Relation>
  </rdf:Description>
</rdf:RDF>
```

This example above shows the different pieces of the RDF. It is a very standard export for exchanging vocabularies.

RDF schemas are similar to XML schemas. A schema defines the meaning, characteristics, and relationships of a set of properties. This may include constraints on potential values and the inheritance of properties from other schemas.

With RDF, a *Resource* is anything that can have a uniform resource identifier (URI). This includes all webpages, and segments of an XML document.

An RDF *PropertyType* is a resource that has a *Name* and can be used as a *Property*. This can be *Author* or *Title*.

An RDF *Property* is the combination of a *Resource*, a *PropertyType*, and a *Value*. For instance, "The Author of http://www.accessinn.com/offkey.htm is Marjorie Hlava." The *Value*, in this case, is "Marjorie Hlava." *Resources* have *Properties*, and *Properties* have *Values*.

Practical uses of RDF include the following:

• website maps

• description of the contents of webpages

• describing the formal structure of privacy practice descriptions

• expressing metadata about metadata

• digital signatures

• thesauri and library classification schemes

Recently, RDF has expanded to include triples for linked data. There is much discussion in the information community about RDF, and most of that discussion is currently linked to triples and linked data. In order to support triples, RDF first needed to be defined as a wrapper. Once we understand the wrapper, we can understand its application in triples. The RDF triple wrapper is used to show the relationship between terms. The most common triple is stated as *object/predicate/subject* or *subject/predicate/object*. As explained by the W3C, "*The underlying structure of any expression in RDF is a collection of triples, each consisting of a subject, a predicate and an object. ... The assertion of an RDF Triple says that some relationship, indicated by the predicate, holds between the things denoted by subject and object of the triple*" (W3C).

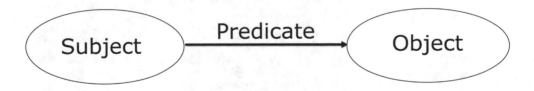

Figure 2.4: Basic structure of the RDF triple metadata wrapper.

RDF is a way to define related term instances. You can have more than one kind of related term. You can do it in an RDF export. You can say "Linda was president of ASIS&T." You can infer other relationships and indicate that "Marjorie Hlava is a member of ASIS&T." RDF triples provide a way to connect different objects and infer or state their relationships, and these can get very complex. The basis of it—RDF was first a wrapper and now has extended that wrapper and the way the syntax works, so that you can talk about it in terms of triples. Triples are the basis of linked data implementations. Taxonomies as subject metadata are an increasingly important part of the linked data world.

2.5   TAXONOMIES IN SHAREPOINT

Many people are interested in SharePoint implementations, perhaps because the SharePoint server comes free with the Microsoft server and can be used to file documents so everyone in the organization can easily find them and work on them collaboratively. I think SharePoint, more than any other thing, has excited interest in taxonomies for people. SharePoint 2010 and SharePoint 2013 have a taxonomy module, and although the module does not have everything that your heart might wish for, it is a significant step forward. A lot of people have been trying to figure out exactly how to best use their taxonomy within the SharePoint offering. This is one option.

Let's step back for a moment and look at the following data flow in general—not just for including with SharePoint.

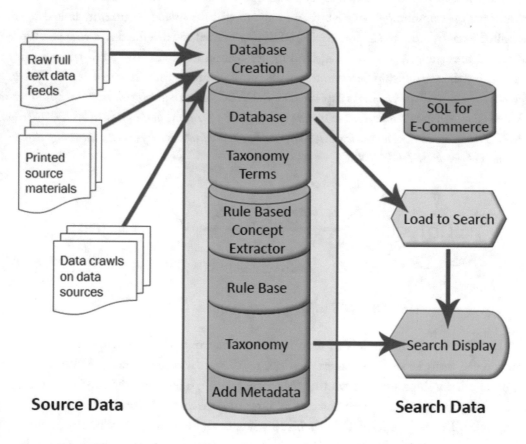

Figure 2.5: Data flow with a taxonomy.

The incoming information needs to be stored in a repository somewhere—your hard drive, shared company drives, somewhere. It would be really nice to add metadata to that repository to enable retrieval by something other than just the file name. Therefore, we want to add taxonomy terms. The taxonomy terms all need to be controlled or suggested. There is a back end application required to make that happen. Once we have the data in that repository, it could be exported to an SQL system, a relational database, or a transactional system for e-commerce or some other use. It might be put into a repository so that the full displays can be made. It might be loaded into a search system. It might have a presentation layer for display.

When possible, it is more efficient to save data to the search and the storage repositories at the same time, so that when you save a record in one place, it saves automatically to all of the other places where you need to have access to that data. That would mean immediate availability of the information to everybody who needs it. You can group this effort to a single production stream that includes mapping your source data, cleaning and enhancing that data, storing it, and making it searchable. You want to be able to get your data, load it and clean it up, and then export it to the several repositories with different requirements, preferably within a single workflow path.

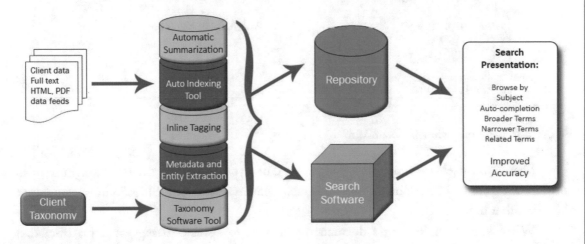

Figure 2.6: A single workflow path provides for maximum efficiency.

SharePoint can support this path with a little augmentation of the SharePoint Term Store function. Begin with your taxonomy, run it through a quality cleanup routine, and store it in the repository. SharePoint actually comes with an embedded search system. Microsoft purchased and offered the Norwegian "FAST Search and Retrieval System" to include as part of SharePoint 2010 and subsequent versions. If your document collection is small, the SharePoint search will work well. If you have a lot of documents, you will need to have something more robust for search—to provide faster query speed and faster results processing. If you add the taxonomy back in at the front end, you can browse and increase the accuracy of the search results. There are a number of options, from Lucene [12] to Perfect Search [13], that you can investigate.

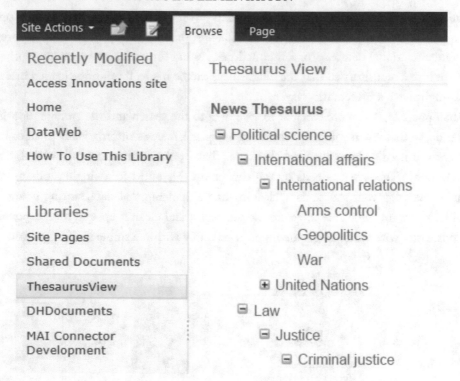

Figure 2.7: Taxonomy view in SharePoint.

SharePoint itself will only show you ten lines of a vocabulary at a time. You might want to consider integrating a taxonomy or thesaurus management system with SharePoint to circumvent this and other limitations.

When you are uploading a document, you want to be able to suggest terms from that document that are valid in your taxonomy and post those as keywords in the SharePoint system so that you can search for them using your taxonomy. Since it is very easy to build a SharePoint application, control of that application can get out of control quickly. People are looking hard to find ways to implement some kind of vocabulary control using SharePoint, particularly the 2010 or 2013 version, and to a lesser extent the 2007 version, so that they can index their documents and retrieve them easily.

Although we do know what a document is about when we file it, it is harder to remember it exactly a few weeks later. If you cannot remember the name of the document when you created it, it is hard to find. Giving it a taxonomy tag set will help in retrieval of the document at a later date. Where you can make broad use of synonyms and browse categories, it is easier to find the information.

People are also trying to use SharePoint for records management. However, because of the nature of records management, you might have groups of record types or facets for record types.

You could also have content types. These record and content types could be put into a taxonomic fashion. You might have human resources documents and under those human resources documents, you might have many different kinds of items, i.e., reviews, résumés, payroll records, and so on. The finance department might also have payroll records, so in your taxonomy you will want have multiple broader terms. Where you have a combination of the record types, the content types, and the creators of those records, you might be able to automate the retention schedule assignments. This is a very heavy load for most organizations these days, to determine the retention schedule for the record types and the content types and keep track of them by creator. How long do you need to keep this particular document, or kind of document? Is it three years for tax audit purposes? Is it seven years for fraud? Do you need to keep them indefinitely for patent research? Do you need at least 17 years to prove copyright provenance? There are many different retention schedules that organizations need to track, and having this kind of automation help from the taxonomy in a Share-Point implementation might be very useful.

2.6   TAXONOMIES AND SEMANTIC INTEGRATION

2.6.1   BREAKING DOWN AUTOMATIC METADATA GENERATION AND EXTRACTION

There are basically two approaches to automatic metadata generation and extraction and within those, many variations.

Statistical Approaches

Statistical approaches use ideas derived from Bayes' theorem [14], neural networks [15], and automatic clustering [16]. An underlying assumption is that words or groups of words that occur together frequently in a big set of data are related conceptually.

Statistical methods depend on algorithms created by a developer, and these algorithms usually include many opportunities for "tuning." Providing access to these tunable components can enhance the system. Statistical systems usually require various forms of "training." For example, the probability of interesting events can be estimated by counting occurrences in a large corpus of data. Interesting events might be events that occur more frequently in your data than in some other set of data. Another approach is to take a list of terms (often a thesaurus, taxonomy, or authority file) and a corpus of text. The system manager processes the inputs, with spot checking and often manual intervention by a human subject matter expert. When the system has been trained, test queries are run on different content to verify that the system is performing as desired.

There are drawbacks in production for statistical methods.

1. Bad data can misguide training algorithms. In order to train the algorithm, you may need to find or create a suitable corpus in which a term is used "correctly." This is expensive and time-consuming, a fact not usually made known to the buyer before the transaction is completed. You might need to process about 300 articles to find 100 articles in which a term is used properly. You can expect to spend at least one hour per term to review the documents and find the right usage for training. Alternatively, you can assume that the bad data is a valid component of your data, accept the bad data as an unavoidable component of real life, and use enough "real" data to subdue the effects of a few "spurious" components. For example, misspelled words occur in real life. Correcting the misspellings might be a lot of work, but they are a "real" component of the data that can be part of the algorithm.

2. When you add new terms to the taxonomy, the meaning and use of a term change. You need to reset the vectors or the statistical values will change. That means that the set needs to be retrained. You may also need to go back to the software vendor and have them do the training of the new sets. Language drift is a normal effect of human communication. Since the drift is slow, retraining can be adjusted to occur slowly also. Incremental adjustments may need to be designed for the training vectors.

3. Statistical systems typically return 40–60% accuracy levels. Accuracy can be improved with better training or with rules, which are discussed below. To avoid this extra step, some statistical systems use a form of relevance ranking based on a confidence factor. The relevance "score" and subsequent ranking are a way of getting around the accuracy measures of precision and recall measured against a vetted set done by human indexers.

The U.S. government, particularly the intelligence community, has been enthralled with the statistical system for years. The government has funded many types of systems, and none of them work particularly well. Early on, In-Q-Tel [17] learned that Stratify (now part of Iron Mountain [18]) was a system that required significant human input. Digital Reasoning's [19] method is an automated process that "discovers" concepts, bound phrases, and entities. In my opinion, neither Stratify nor Digital Reasoning delivers a slam dunk.

To find the words to create the training sets takes more time than developing a taxonomy. Once found, the set needs to be trained, and if any new word co-occurrences are discovered, they cannot be trained alone like a taxonomy term. The entire corpus needs to be rerun and retrained, and this can take weeks. While that is happening, the bad guys are changing their terms again— they know how long it takes to retrain, so they stay ahead of the system. It makes it easy for the bad guys and really tough for the intelligence analysts to keep up. In fact, I think this circumstance has led to massive intelligence failures.

Vendors in this space have been heavily financed by the government. The statistical approach also has become the pet of some university researchers, because they can get their Ph.D. and start their own data mining business or get hired by a government contractor and benefit from that "heavy financing," or they can get a grant from the government and support their faculty position.

There is a lot of overlap between the statistical systems for data mining systems and the search vendors that depend on the same kinds of processing. Auto indexing vendors using statistics-based systems include Coveo [20], Clearview [21], ClearForest [22], JustSystems [23], and TEMIS [24]. Search vendors using statistics include Google and HP Autonomy [25].

Rule-Based Approaches

The second approach to automatic metadata generation and extraction is rule-based. These systems also start with a list of terms, for example, a thesaurus, taxonomy, or authority file. These systems build rules of two types: (1) simple (match and identity) rules, or if Term A, use term A, and if Synonym B, use Term A, which support about 80% of the terms and may be automatically created; and (2) complex rules (including conditions beyond the initial text to match). The complexity of the rules can vary considerably [26].

One of the greatest benefits of rule-based systems is that they provide consistent suggestions. The suggestion of a term is the same every time under the same conditions in a computer-assisted indexing engine, if it is a rule-based system. The system behaves differently if it is statistically based, whether it is a Bayesian, neural network, co-occurrence, or other kind of statistical system.

Once the suggested indexing from a rule-based system is presented to the indexer or keyword tagger, he or she may look at the results of automatic indexing, or at least review a sample of the output. The computer will do exactly what you told it to do. You may have heard the adage, "Listen to what I'm thinking instead of what I said." Computers pay attention to what you tell them, and only to exactly what you tell them. They don't listen to what you're thinking, and they can provide some amusing results.

The next thing we want to do is measure the accuracy of the indexing presented using our taxonomy, whether it is applied solely by human effort with computer assistance, or entirely by computer. We are able to measure consistency: whether or not the same terms are applied under the same conditions to different records. We measure against human indexing, which is normally called a "vetted set," a set of data that has already been indexed. There are three pillars of this measurement, *Hits*, *Misses*, and *Noise*. A *Hit* is a term that the human would assign and that is suggested by the system. A *Miss* is a term that the machine did not suggest but that the human did assign. *Noise* is a term that the machine assigned but the human did not. Sometimes the *noise* may actually be a good indexing term that the human missed, so some systems will subdivide the results into relevant and irrelevant noise. Relevant noise is the "good" indexing that the human missed. Once a set of relevant noise is established, it can also be used to assess the efficacy of a human indexing team.

Testing the rules against the data could be considered training the rules. It means that we take a test batch of data, process it through the rules, and have a human indexer review the results. We add the complex rules for those terms for which the *noise* and *misses* are high.

The differences among the vendors in this space come down to how long it takes to build a rule and whether the vendor has a thesaurus/taxonomy tool. That is the real cost of implementation, because with rule-based systems, humans have to create the rules. Google has automated systems that generate changes to rules, so once there are some rules, humans are freed up to do other things. This is a key advantage that Google has, but as far as I know they have not yet leveraged it in a way that generates revenue. Endeca [27], recently acquired by Oracle, is at the foundation level in terms of human indexing and rules for these kinds of systems.

Auto-indexing (also known as auto categorization or autocat) systems and vendors using rule-based methods include Data Harmony's M.A.I. and MAIstro [28], Teragram [29], and partially SmartLogic [30]. Search vendors using rules or faceted search systems include Endeca and possibly Exalead [31]. Exalead is similar to Google in that it is a hybrid system. The Perfect Search Corporation uses a system that works as an accelerator for relational database queries.

Statistical Rule-Based Systems

Most systems end up being hybrid systems. They start as one and then embrace the useful parts of the other point of view to make a workable product. In the hybrid product of Bayesian, statistical systems and rule-based systems, probabilities can be associated with rules, and then a probability can be associated with each classification. The system I work with is the Data Harmony system, which has two levels. First is the natural language processing (NLP) layer, which applies what it can to the words in a parsing engine. However, early research showed that most NLP systems, automated language processing (ALP) systems in general, and Bayesian systems needed to add rules to get them beyond a 40–60% accuracy rate. We found that about 80% of the terms only required simple rules either to directly match the text string or to direct the system to use a synonym of that term.

IF "automobiles" USE "automobiles." That is, if the term in the text and in the taxonomy as the preferred term is automobiles, and that is what is in the source content—well, then, that's what you use.

To match the synonyms is easy as well. IF "cars" USE "automobiles." With this methodology we can reach about 80% accuracy quickly using match and identity rules. This led us to develop a rules system that could be used by the bench editor to customize the word base application to their specific content. We added additional syntax for the more complex relationships in an engine so that the system could return automatically in the mid-90 percent range for accuracy. This felt like a good region and matched at least the human effort, and editorial drift problems were solved as well.

Some hybrid systems started from a Bayesian approach and hit the 60% wall and so added rules either as SQL rules or through training processes to reach the higher accuracies needed for production-level implementations. GrapeVine and Nstein were able to use a variation on the same syntax to develop the rules part of their system. Smartlogic first went with a pure statistical approach but added rules system quickly. Temis also went with training in a Bayesian system, and moved to a combination of training and SQL rules. The challenge with the SQL rules is that they need to be built by a programmer and are usually provided by the vendor. It means that the customer is not able to easily add terms to the taxonomy in conjunction with the accompanying auto-indexing component. They must go to their autocat vendor to get the terms added and trained.

Comparing the Approaches

For a comparison of rules-based and statistical approaches to automated indexing, see the author's article, "Automatic Indexing: Comparing Rule-based and Statistics-Based Indexing Systems," *Information Outlook*, Volume 9, Number 8 (August 2005), pages 22–23. This article is republished at http://taxodiary.com/2010/12/automatic-indexing-how-two-approaches-compare/.

2.7   INDEXING VS. HIERARCHY

The indexing of the content depends only on the terms themselves and their synonyms. The related terms and broader–narrower relationships are great for managing the taxonomy and for presentation and a search interface, but they are completely independent of the use of the terms in indexing. Automatic indexing systems like Data Harmony's M.A.I. treat the terms as though they are all on an equal level. The placement in the hierarchy is irrelevant to the term usage in the indexing process.

Just as indexers have always done in the past, and the NISO Z39.14 standard recommends, you should generally index to the most specific level. The term *Transportation*, for example, is applied where it is appropriate to the content. There is no hierarchy implied by using a top-level term for indexing. It is simply that the article or item mentioned is a broad paper and cannot be more specifically indexed or tagged with a lower taxonomy term.

Now, that said, I am sympathetic to the unending repetition of the terms in the index. It becomes unwieldy. But each unit is indexed only according to the content it contains. Something with a transportation title in a state code may really only have to do with road works, so it does not need transportation applied to it, while an industry-wide report on the state of transportation in the country would be appropriately tagged as transportation.

When you display the records using the hierarchy, all things having to do with transportation will be apparent and clear to the users. Take a look at MediaSleuth [32]—there is a browseable navigation tree on the left side. Each record is attached according to the terms used to index it.

There are two sides to this coin—the application of specific terms to the records of content at all levels according to their specific (or at the chapter level broad) content, and the display of that data in the user interface. Use the related term for indexing if it is the most appropriate term.

2.7.1 CHANGING THE HIERARCHY

The hierarchy is the network of the relationships among the terms. You can display the same information—the same set of taxonomy terms—in many different ways. The fact that the hierarchy is going to depend on your view of the field also means that when you are focusing on some particular collection, some particular group of information, you might want to change the hierarchy. You aren't changing the terms; instead, you are using the same terms underneath to index the corpus. However, the way it is displayed, the way it is presented to the user, is going to depend on which group's needs you are trying to accommodate.

For instance, if you have two million items in your collection, you might decide that you want to make a new subset of those items. You run your automatic indexing on those documents and bring together those that have the right subject terms for review. Then you look at the current taxonomy suggested by what's left—because not everything in the collection, and therefore not all of the words in your taxonomy, will be used. That much smaller collection will leave you with a residual set of terms. You may look at them and say, "You know, for this set of people, for the Spanish Studies people, I am going to present a different collection than I had for those interested in world wars. A lot of the documents will be the same, but I will present them in a really different fashion." For a different purpose or a different group of people, you want to organize the information differently. You might be tagging it the same way and using the same thesaurus to tag it, but with a product development point of view, you've come up with an entirely new offering for your users, even though you are still using the same set of data. There are many things that can be done with a thesaurus, and this is one example of something you might want to do.

When we change the organization of government, we change the entire organization of the Superintendent of Documents collection because we're following the outline of the new government. New people come in and they think of something in a different way, and they change the hierarchy of the classification system, but the documents that are in the collection remain the same. Fortunately, those documents are indexed with a subject catalog so we can still get to the documents we want.

We don't need to worry about the classification system in order to find our desired documents. Don't get so hung up on the hierarchy that you forget that you can change it tomorrow.

CHAPTER 3

How is a Taxonomy Connected to Search?

3.1   THE WORLD OF SEARCH

Search is such a wonderful and widely debated issue. The world of search is ever-changing and fascinating to watch as developments continue.

Search is sometimes like having to stand in a long line waiting to order a cold drink on a hot day. You want the drink but hate the line, and what if the person pouring the drinks gets your order wrong? You'll have to start all over. There will always be dissatisfaction because "search" stands between you and the information you want. That said, I think the reason that indexing with a controlled vocabulary (such as a taxonomy or thesaurus) is so popular compared to the use of free ranging keywords is the degree of control obtained not just in the indexing, but also in search. The taxonomy approach is like placing your drink order efficiently. You know what you want, and how to convey that to the server—whether the server is providing your cold drink, or offering up your search results—and what you receive in the end satisfies your needs.

I think that, with a couple of rare exceptions, search itself has not made many recent advances. Under the hood in search, things like new caching algorithms, faster stemming, and co-occurrence indications are rather esoteric and don't make much news. The advances have mainly been in the user experience. The layer between the technology infrastructure and the web display is where the action resides. The user interface also plays a very important part in search. There have been significant improvements over the past decade or so in this aspect of search.

3.2   DISPLAYING CONTENT BASED ON SEARCH: AN ASSOCIATION EXAMPLE

Professional associations need to serve a great deal of content to their members on their web and journal distribution sites. If one taxonomy is used to tag all the content, then the appropriate material, regardless of type, can be delivered through the content management system (CMS) each time the taxonomy terms are used in a search query. The main information is delivered with the collateral information at the same time, giving a rich search and user experience.

If you use your taxonomy to index everything in your corpus and on your website, then you are in a good position to present your content to your users. Using the same term list overall allows you to show related content in many ways. You could link content by journal article, which is a common linking activity, because articles on the same subjects would be linked by common terms. You could also link content by activity. If people are working on an activity, you could direct their attention to another activity or a resource that is likely to be of interest to them.

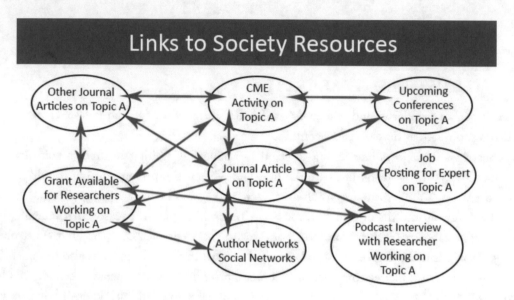

Figure 3.1: Diagram of relationships between various resources common to professional and scholarly societies. The original of this image was presented by Helen Atkins during her presentation at the 2012 DHUG (Data Harmony Users Group) meeting.

For example, a search on "nanotechnology" would bring up papers on the topic and in the surrounding areas on the webpage that show related research, upcoming conferences, job postings, grant opportunities, and so forth, all on the topic of nanotechnology. The posted job openings on the search topic add to the richness of the search encounter as would ads supplied. The information presented comes from several different databases or data streams but is all conceptually appropriate to the search topic.

Perhaps you have a podcast interview in which someone is talking on the subject that a searcher just entered, and that would also be of interest to them. Maybe there are other people who are working in the same field as you who have profiled themselves with that same taxonomy term; you could provide them with ways of contacting other people they might want to connect with in a social networking opportunity or for scientific collaboration. There are many ways to expose additional related and useful information based on the taxonomy terms. Many websites do this with advertising now, presenting marketing content based on your search queries.

The screenshot below, from the website of the American Association for Cancer Research [33], shows some of these capabilities. The searcher has found a communication in a journal on Cancer Epidemiology, Biomarkers, and Prevention. A set of keywords is included in the search results display, indicating what content the organization can offer them, based on the terms entered for the search. The searcher might be interested in particular working groups, or awards, think tank reports, some webcasts, or maybe some related book content, and the search results display includes links to listing of that content. In this particular case, further links could even take you to a book chapter that has to do with your subjects, abstracts from upcoming conferences that might be useful, some workshops and other conferences that are being held on the topics and where they are, and even press releases. If you have linked the resources behind the scenes, by indexing them all using your taxonomy, then you can offer many different kinds of related content in many different ways.

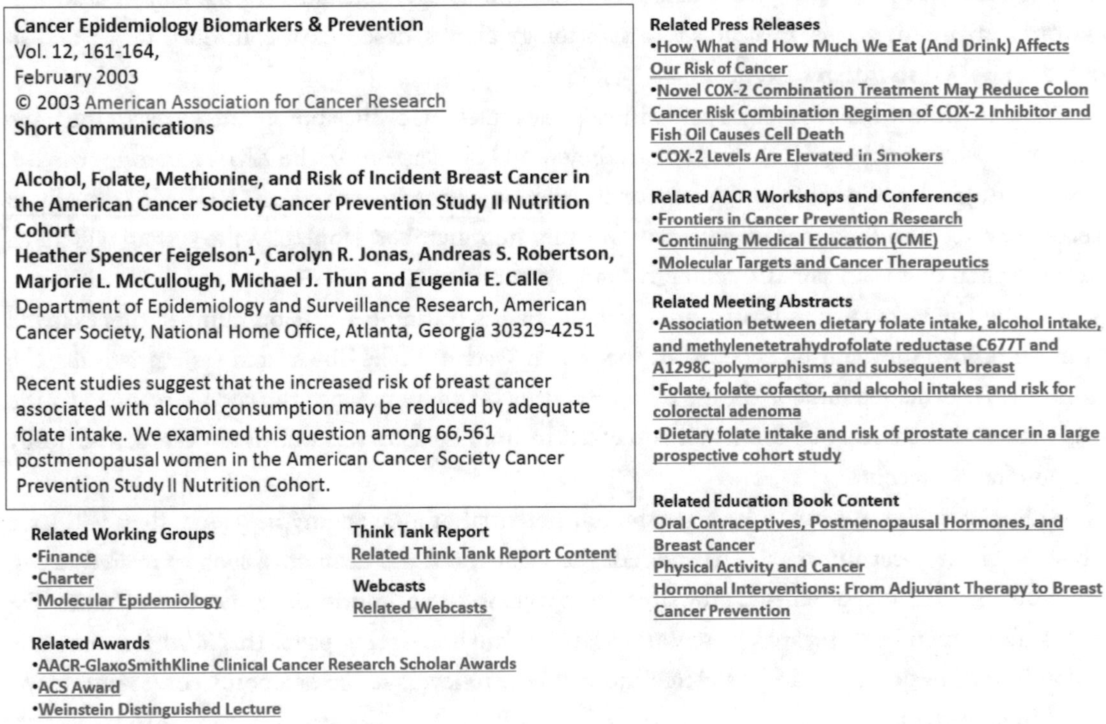

Cancer Epidemiology Biomarkers & Prevention
Vol. 12, 161-164,
February 2003
© 2003 American Association for Cancer Research
Short Communications

Alcohol, Folate, Methionine, and Risk of Incident Breast Cancer in the American Cancer Society Cancer Prevention Study II Nutrition Cohort
Heather Spencer Feigelson[1], Carolyn R. Jonas, Andreas S. Robertson, Marjorie L. McCullough, Michael J. Thun and Eugenia E. Calle
Department of Epidemiology and Surveillance Research, American Cancer Society, National Home Office, Atlanta, Georgia 30329-4251

Recent studies suggest that the increased risk of breast cancer associated with alcohol consumption may be reduced by adequate folate intake. We examined this question among 66,561 postmenopausal women in the American Cancer Society Cancer Prevention Study II Nutrition Cohort.

Related Working Groups
•Finance
•Charter
•Molecular Epidemiology

Related Awards
•AACR-GlaxoSmithKline Clinical Cancer Research Scholar Awards
•ACS Award
•Weinstein Distinguished Lecture

Think Tank Report
Related Think Tank Report Content

Webcasts
Related Webcasts

Related Press Releases
•How What and How Much We Eat (And Drink) Affects Our Risk of Cancer
•Novel COX-2 Combination Treatment May Reduce Colon Cancer Risk Combination Regimen of COX-2 Inhibitor and Fish Oil Causes Cell Death
•COX-2 Levels Are Elevated in Smokers

Related AACR Workshops and Conferences
•Frontiers in Cancer Prevention Research
•Continuing Medical Education (CME)
•Molecular Targets and Cancer Therapeutics

Related Meeting Abstracts
•Association between dietary folate intake, alcohol intake, and methylenetetrahydrofolate reductase C677T and A1298C polymorphisms and subsequent breast
•Folate, folate cofactor, and alcohol intakes and risk for colorectal adenoma
•Dietary folate intake and risk of prostate cancer in a large prospective cohort study

Related Education Book Content
Oral Contraceptives, Postmenopausal Hormones, and Breast Cancer
Physical Activity and Cancer
Hormonal Interventions: From Adjuvant Therapy to Breast Cancer Prevention

Figure 3.2: Website with links to additional suggested resources for the searcher.

3.3   HOW IS A TAXONOMY CONNECTED TO SEARCH?

A customer asked me, "How is the taxonomy connected to search?" This is such a seemingly simple question with a long answer. That is why I have named both this chapter and this section with that very question.

The taxonomy (the hierarchical view of a controlled vocabulary) is really just a list of terms in their preferred form to be used to index individual articles or papers in a collection. The indexed items can be books, book chapters, journal articles, museum specimens, white papers, technical reports, HR documents, payroll records, really anything that needs to be retrieved or pulled back out of the computer system. Let's call them "information objects," IO. The same situation arises when items are loaded to a records management system (RMS) or a content management system (CMS), SharePoint, or a library catalog (OPAC [34]). Each application calls the activity of indexing and its products something different, which makes our lives confusing. Metadata tagging, subject headings, keywords, taxonomy terms, thesaurus terms, ontology classes, descriptors, controlled terms, and so forth are all used in different venues.

The workflow has two major parts. First is the attaching of the appropriate terms to the individual information objects (IO). That means they would be elements in the XML record for the IO. They also might be in a table in the relational database management system (RDBMS), usually as a secondary key and linked to an accession or other item number. Hopefully, the system will allow you more than one term per IO, although some systems don't.

Once the terms are indicated, attached, or share a common accession number, then, second in our workflow, they can be accessed in the search system. Voilà! The search system is using the taxonomy! Another example is the use of a UPC code on an item. Once the code is scanned by the UPC reader at the checkout counter, it is tracked in store inventory as well as appears semantically on a purchaser's receipt.

However, if you want to leverage the full potential of a taxonomy in search, then you have to have it on the user interface (UI) end. All the wonders of the taxonomy, such as related terms, synonyms, hierarchy, type-ahead, browsing the navigation tree, and recommendations ("more like these"), all happen in the search presentation layer of the user-facing page. This is where some understanding of basic information architecture and how to leverage the taxonomy comes into play.

In summary,

- the taxonomy is used to tag records to provide meaningful subject access to the records;

- the search software incorporates the taxonomy terms in the inverted file of the retrieval engine, not visible to a searcher;

- the taxonomy is showcased on the user experience or search interface where the user can browse, get additional suggestions, and be prompted to do a better search by leveraging the taxonomy terms and relationships; and,

- to use the search presentation layer, the interface is really interacting with two things simultaneously. It is sending the search query to the search software indexes and caches and at the same time, it is sending the term searched for to the taxonomy interface to surface additional taxonomy terms. These additional terms might be related terms and/or narrower terms that show part of the navigation hierarchy. The interaction also enables the type-ahead feature. The "type-ahead feature" is essentially the same as the auto-complete feature mentioned earlier.

3.4   USING A TAXONOMY TO GUIDE THE SEARCHER

Figure 3.3: View of www.mediasleuth.com with the taxonomy hierarchy on the left, the browseable categories at the top right, a search function, expand or narrow your search options, and the top few results for the selected term.

The image above shows the taxonomy hierarchy on the left. In this example, the user can navigate the full taxonomic tree, opening and collapsing branches as preferred. In this example, there are numbers after the terms. The numbers tell the user how many records are tagged with those terms in the corpus, in the database or set of information covered. All of that information is visible and available to the user to indicate exactly how much content is in each of those branches. Studying such a display is a good way, if you are building a taxonomy, to get a feel for how many terms are over-loaded and how many of these terms have zero or few articles indexed using them, in which case they might not be sensible taxonomy terms.

Another way to use the taxonomy in search is to combine the synonyms as well as the main terms and display them in a permuted list. In a permuted list, the multi-word phrase terms are displayed in alphabetical order, once for each of the words in each term. For example, Sickle cell disease would be found as the same heading under Disease and under Sickle. The searcher shouldn't have to know exactly what term the taxonomist finally decided to use as the primary term in the taxonomy. Using type-ahead based on the permuted index, they could just type in a word and they would have a good idea of the term options surrounding that concept. If they click on the term, it would automatically implement the search.

In Figure 3.3 above, you will notice contextually appropriate terms under Expand Your Search. These links show the related terms for the search term as an expansion of the search option. Narrower terms are also displayed so that the user can narrow the search and make it more specific. These three highlighted examples show ways to guide the user on the search side directly from the taxonomy itself. These were created from the term record in the full thesaurus using those relationships to leverage search.

My observations suggest that people are able to do a search much faster if they can use browseable categories. Dumais, Cutrell, and Chen and have written a perceptive study on how helpful it is, concluding: "*Participants liked the category interface much better than the list interface, and they were 50% faster in finding information that was organized into categories*" [35]. Searchers have many different learning styles, and therefore they have different ways to search. However, if you offer a browseable category search, some users will certainly prefer it to other options.

3.5   TOOLS FOR SEARCH

Search engines, technology related to them (including web crawlers and search software), and getting those things implemented to put taxonomies to good use are important but complex topics. It follows on the question of "Now that we have the taxonomy—NOW WHAT?" It is crucial for taxonomists to understand the pieces of the puzzle, so that they can get their work into production and use.

3.5.1   SEARCH ENGINES

A search *engine* is different from search software. The terms are used interchangeably by many people, but they are not at all the same. Search *software* is a software application, while a search engine is a collection of servers with a large amount of data stored, computer-indexed, and searchable on the Internet. Search engines deliver HTML pages to customers through their search engine technology and are usually supported by ad revenue. The search engines explore the sites across the Internet to gather content, often from metadata in the HTML headers, and increasingly from full text accessible on the Internet. The search engines load that information, compare it, rank it, and allow users to search it. If you've done searches using Google [36], Bing [37], Yahoo [38], Ask.com [39], or AOL [40], you have some firsthand experience with this process.

3.5.2   CRAWLERS AND SPIDERS

A crawler or spider is a software application that is programmed and scheduled to explore specific intranet or Internet pages, plus pages to which those pages are hyperlinked. A crawler that explores Internet pages is known as a web crawler or web spider. Upon reaching the destination pages, a crawler extracts whatever kind of information it is programmed to capture. It then deposits that information in the search engine application so that it can be searched. What it really stores is the location of the information, generally the URL, the keywords, and perhaps other information in the HTML headers. It might also pull the content of the entire page and cache it someplace so that it can be displayed quickly; however, this is not as common.

Crawlers are connected to the website visibility for your organization. Creating metadata for crawlers to find is fairly straightforward. Without metadata, structure, and categorization, web crawlers have nothing to work on. If you don't have the metadata and the structured information and the keywords applied to your web content, the crawlers can't work well, and your information is not as discoverable as it could be. We need that metadata so that the crawlers or spiders can sort out information on the web in an organized way.

The metadata tags are the first place on a webpage that the crawler mines for information. Crawlers depend on the information in the metadata header fields to know whether to mine the page further. Generally, they crawl first to the metadata header text and harvest what they can, and then the crawler's software algorithm makes a decision about whether to mine the page further and perhaps where to place it in the ranked search results. If the crawler doesn't find the kind of information it's looking for in the metadata, it will go deeper down on the page, but the page will be lower-ranked because the information was not as easy to find. Then the algorithm determines if the system will cache the page or not, and whether they are going to cache just the first page or the entire site. Crawlers might go through a site every two weeks, but there might be some newer sites that they crawl more frequently, perhaps every 15 minutes.

Having the appropriate information in the HTML header metadata fields determines how the crawlers will treat the website. The downside is that if it finds the same keyword used multiple times in the meta name="keywords" fields, the crawler may recognize that as a rank-boosting tactic and consequently rank the page lower because of it. If I have the word "taxonomies" in my HTML header metadata, and I want my webpage to rank high in search results for "taxonomies" queries, I might be tempted to repeat that word several times in my meta name="keywords" field. That would be an error on my part. I should instead repeat the word "taxonomies" in the full text of many pages on my site.

3.5.3   SEARCH SOFTWARE

Search *software* looks at one or more discrete collections of articles, images, and/or the like, which could be huge. Search software is likely to be applied to internal collections or on a single website for the content residing there.

There are dozens of search software systems available. A few examples of search software are MicrosoftSharePoint/FAST [41], the Google Search Appliance [42], Amazon CloudSearch [43] HP Autonomy [44], Attivio [45], Endeca [46], LucidWorks [47], Vivisimo [48], Sinequa [49], NXT/Folio [50], and some open source alternatives such as Solr Lucene [51] and ElasticSearch [52].

3.6   PARTS OF A SEARCH-CAPABLE SYSTEM

In the section above, I talk about the tools needed for a search system, specifically, software components. In this section, I present several items that form the technical basis of a search-capable system. Most systems will normally include at least some, if not all, of the items described below.

3.6.1   RANKING ALGORITHMS

Ranking algorithms enable a system to provide search results data in a sequence that is most likely to answer the query of the user or the search question. The ranking algorithms determine what items should be put higher in the returned results queue.

3.6.2   QUERY LANGUAGE AND SYNTAX

A query language and syntax provide a set of conventions that enable you to actually ask a question of a computer, in a form that the computer can understand. This is what someone is going to use to get a result. The query language usually has two levels. One level captures what the user types into a box, and then in the second level that typed information is translated into a command line that is sent to the search software itself.

3.6.3   A FEDERATOR

Federators may be used to divide up large files into portions to bring the results back more quickly through parallel processing, or they may pull information from several different databases in different locations searched simultaneously, using connectors to untangle the different protocols in use to return a unified set of results. If you are planning to do "federated search" [53], one that provides a unified view of search results from multiple databases, websites, or repositories, you will need some kind of federator, either as on-premises software or as a service. This could be (1) a *query federator*, which rewrites search queries into a form that can be passed along to and understood by federated search engines, or (2) a *content federator*, which gathers the information from various places and puts it into a single cache to be searched.

3.6.4   CACHES AND CACHING ALGORITHMS

The cache of a computer is a component that stores data in a form that makes that data easily accessible to a browser or search engine. This data is copied from the regular data storage. Having the copied data on hand makes it quicker to retrieve, without having to go back to the original. The local cache is also useful if the original data is no longer available. The data in a cache is often handled in an intermediate processing step. Cached data may be stored for speed of display, which is why you need to ask your browser to refresh a page for the most recent data and version from the database or host search system. It allows the system to "buy time" by showing the user something from the cache while the current information is loading.

A caching algorithm works behind the scenes. When you search on a query, it displays the results from the cache. It starts by displaying the first ten or so results, rather than displaying the full quantity of results in the small amount of memory partition that has been allocated to you behind the scenes. As you go through the pages presented, it caches the next page in line so that it is ready when you click on that next page. However, not all of the pages are ready. If you go to the last number in the list, it takes a while longer to get that information to the screen—the algorithm has to go through all the intermediate caching following the algorithms for ranking and display before it can show those to you. It is queuing up the other information in case you want it. The caching algorithm will only go slightly in advance of the original query, in order to not take up more memory than it needs to. Cache memory and the results of caching aspects of a search system help it work and serve the results to the user more quickly.

3.6.5   AN INVERTED INDEX

Once you have ranking algorithms, a query language and syntax, a federator, and a caching algorithm. Most search software builds an inverted index—an alphabetical sort of every term in the searchable areas that you will be covering. There are other approaches, but they are rare and tend to be much less efficient than the inverted index approach.

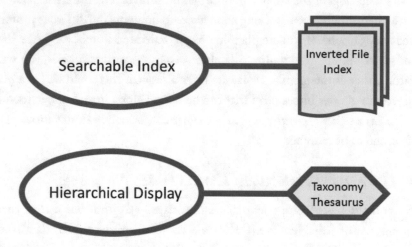

Figure 3.4: The inverted index creates a searchable index, whereas a taxonomy or thesaurus provides only the hierarchical display. Both functions are important in a search-capable system.

The inverted index is something that is basic to practically all search systems. It is the alphabetic or alphanumeric listing of every word, and connections with those words for everything that is searchable in the database. If a word is not in the inverted index, it is not in the searchable file. The inverted index is an important thing for practically all searches.

One alternative to the inverted index is a string search that plows through the entire corpus of files from beginning to end, looking for a string that matches your search query exactly. This is a very slow process, so the almost universal application of inverted indexes is a much more reasonable approach.

3.6.6   THE PRESENTATION LAYER

The presentation layer is what you see on the screen—it is the user interface to access the search capability. The search function may be just a small box you type something into, or it may be an "advanced search" page that provides all the various options for matching your query to the search system underneath. There is no way to tell by looking at the search box itself how the search is implemented underneath. This diagram of a search system shows how the presentation layer might be connected to other components of a search-capable system.

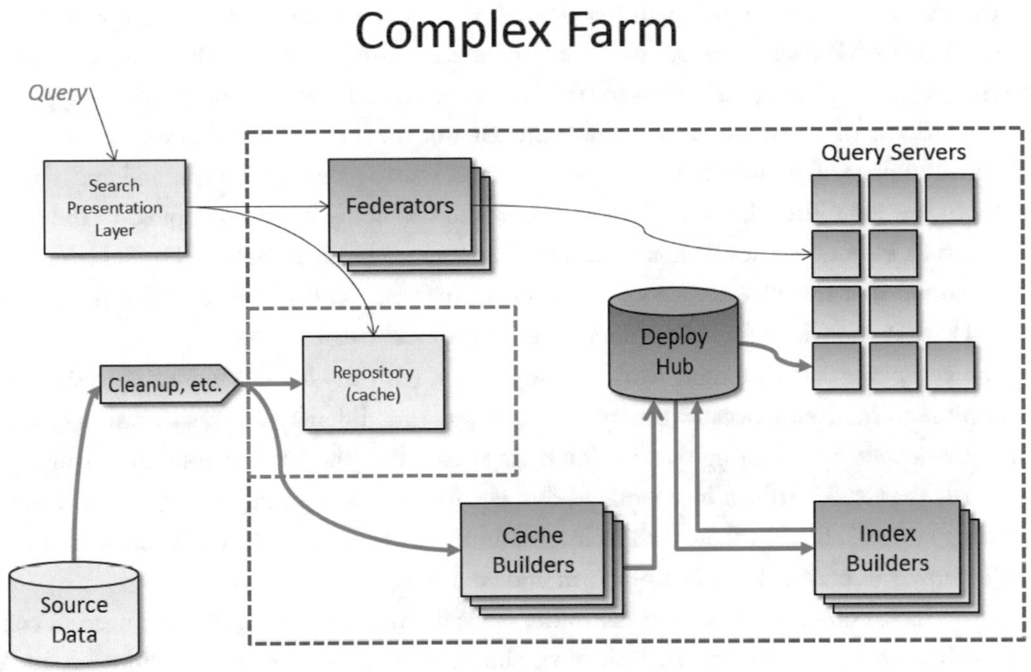

Complex Farm

Figure 3.5: The presentation layer—user interface—of the Perfect Search system is what the user sees. The workings of search that underlie the system are connected but invisible to the user.

You might notice that in this diagram, the presentation layer is working in two places at the same time. The user is able to search the federator and the cache repository at the same time. The federator is taking the search out to all of the query servers, and looking at data in several different places. At the same time, the cache, where the information might have come from the source data—with some cleanup algorithms to make sure that it presents properly going into the cache—is also being searched. The information from both actions is going into the cache builders, then into both the deploy hub and the index builders, which is where the inverted file is built. All of this information, through the query servers and through the federators, is coming back and giving the users their answers. There is an extraordinary amount of activity going on behind the little search box.

3.6.7 SOME VARIABLES

The parts of search are somewhat variable—every system does it a little differently. There's the search software, based on one of two major theoretical camps (Bayesian and Boolean). Then, there's the computer network that the search software is based on. Then, there's the way that the text is parsed—read by a computer to identify where individual words, sentences, and the like begin and end—which is not always the same.

There's also a differentiation between whether the search is working on well-formed or structured text. With XML, we talk about well-formed data, essentially meaning that the data is tagged consistently and will pass a parsing test for the XML structure. However, not all XML-tagged text is metadata. Some of those tags are for the formatting of the document and assistance in rendering the printed page. They might indicate, for instance, where paragraphs begin and end, chapters begin, footnotes are inserted, etc. It is possible that the taxonomy has been applied to the data as part of the data structure. The taxonomy terms can be included in the structured or field-formatted data. Be warned that the advertisements about processing your unstructured text into miraculously structured text at the click of a button are just as they appear—disingenuous.

The computer software must work in conjunction with the hardware. Not everything runs on every piece of hardware, because the operating systems are different. Some software is compiled to run under a specific operating system. The main reason that the Java programming language is so popular is that it is platform independent, that is, programs written in Java can run on a variety of operating systems. Finally, there is the telecommunications system or network connection to the system, or how you access the search platform and your data.

If you have chosen to go a Bayesian route, as we discussed in Chapter 2, you need to collect training sets so that the statistical analysis of the indexing system has something to work on. You need at least 20 records, and 100 are better, for each taxonomy term or concept you want to train the system to search. In these records, the term must be used correctly, with no allowance for metaphor or other creative expression. Our experience has shown us that you need to collect at least 20 records for each term, because words and phrases can be used in many ways.

Search software is built in different ways. Figure 3.6 shows an example.

This is an example showing the FAST search software, which was bought by Microsoft. In FAST, the crawlers look for appropriate information and bring that information into the system. FAST can also bring in the information through file traversers [54] and API connectors to other data systems. For example, it could be indexing all of the emails and other data coming from Oracle, Documentum, FileNet, and some other big systems, going through content application programming interfaces (APIs). This API is translating all of the information that came in from other collections into the form that FAST can process. It is building a cache and then loading the information into what FAST calls a document processor or what Perfect Search Corporation calls a deploy hub.

When the data lands here, it is an ideal time to apply the taxonomy terms to the data. In FAST, we suggest adding the taxonomy terms in the document processor if they are not already on the documents themselves. Adding them at this point means that information will be included in the building of the inverted file and the indexed database, and can be used in search. FAST may also build another database to support sending out alerts and RSS feeds [55] and the like. Putting the taxonomy terms in the inverted index means that they can be sent out with, or used to tailor, those alerts.

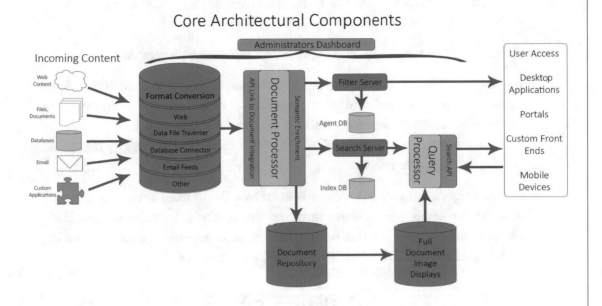

Figure 3.6: Diagram of how a search in FAST might be processed.

This information—the inverted index—is searchable through a query made using the presentation layer. That query is where the user is coming in from. Whether the users are accessing the system on a mobile device, a desktop computer, or a laptop computer, all are gaining access through the query processor. If you also apply the taxonomy terms at the query end in the search presentation layer, you will have a better search experience.

3.7   ASSEMBLING A SEARCH-CAPABLE SYSTEM

Below are some basics for putting together a search system. For technical details, discuss these items with your technical personnel.

- Design the system application. This step includes selection of the fields or elements for the data to reside in. For each of those elements, decide on their desired behavior: mandatory or not, multiple entry allowed, is there a pick list to supply or a taxonomy to call for that element, are there only some characters or a range of values allowed within the element? And so forth.

- Look at the data and decide what needs to be added to enhance it. This is where the taxonomy comes in, for enhancing data by adding taxonomy terms or subject metadata.

- Consider what metadata, other data, and other controls your system needs in order to work properly.

- Once you have done all that, find a system that will work with your data.

- You need at least one database element in the record or schema to contain the subject metadata. Don't work for months on a schema just to find out that when you try to stuff your data into the schema, you forgot to allow for multiple terms or multiple authors, or you forgot to add pagination. I have seen cases of all of these omissions and they are frustrating to resolve.

- Research search software. Many organizations have five or more kinds of search software. All too often, none of them work and this is why they end up with so many, several of which are just sitting on the shelf. These organizations aren't determining the needs of the data first and selecting search software second.

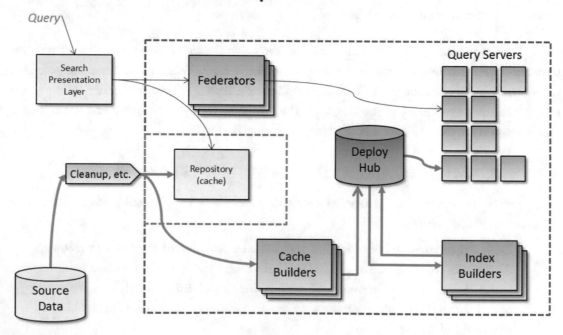

Figure 3.7: Source data flow in the Perfect Search system.

- I believe in the data first. We used the above diagram earlier in this chapter, but now we are going to examine how the source data flows in this process. For this flow to work, your data must be in a uniform format. This is often called the conversion process or the ETL—extract, transform, and load—process.

- Next, the clean and uniform data needs to be deposited into a cache or repository of the data. It might be held in a content management system (CMS), as in the diagram above. Next you will build a way to access the repository in the cache builders. After that, the data goes into some kind of a hub to deploy that information into search. From the hub, the inverted file indexes are built, so that you have those indexes available for searching.

- The user will submit queries into the search presentation layer. If you have multiple repositories that you want to search across, you will need a federator, which will be connected to the query servers that will access the deploy hub, access the indexes, and return results to the user.

- The content that then comes into the system has to be digested by the system. It is digested by an assortment of connectors or conversion programs that then load it into the content API for the search software.

- The document is processed—broken down into pieces—so that the search system can use it. For managing full articles, the system has to have a server. It will have an index so that you can show the individual files, and it might have filters for sending out alerts and RSS feeds to different kinds of receiving organizations.

- When the user submits a query, the search request is moving through a query API— or a search application protocol interface—something that will translate the search question into the syntax within the system. It goes into the query processor and then accesses the inner workings of the system, the inverted file.

- The taxonomy can come into play in two parts—the taxonomy governance layer and the search or query end of the system.

With a taxonomy governance layer, an ideal option, apply the taxonomy terms to documents as they are processed into the system, or at least somewhere along the document-processing pipeline. If you are lucky, you can also use the taxonomy at the search end so that people can disambiguate their queries as they are searching the system. Taxonomy, to my mind, should be in both of these places within your search implementation. Really, search is the reason you built the taxonomy in the first place.

3.8   MEASURING QUALITY IN SEARCH

Search quality involves several different factors, including accuracy, speed, and usability.

3.8.1   SEARCH ACCURACY

People talk about how "accurate" a search is. When a search system ranks results, showing you the ones that it determines to be the best first, the system is guessing which results are most likely to be accurate, and which are more likely to be accurate than others. There are many different ways to measure search accuracy. This list indicates some of the ways that information professionals discuss measuring search accuracy.

- Relevance

- Recall

- Precision

- Hits, misses, and noise

- Ranking

- Query processing speed

- Results processing speed

- Display

- Search refinement

- Usability

- Business rules

As you can see from this list, there are many different aspects of accuracy one might focus on. Relevance has become extraordinarily popular, so I put that at the top, but there are many other ways to measure accuracy.

Relevance is a measure of how well the documents answer your needs. It is a very subjective measure and it is different for different user communities. It really depends on the information resources and the tension between the user needs and the context available. It is possible that there is nothing relevant to your search in the entire corpus.

Recall is the measure of how many of the records in the database match your query versus how many you actually got. If you are a doctoral student or a patent researcher, or a litigator looking for a smoking gun document in a legal case, you might want 100% recall. If you are simply looking for a discussion of a topic or a quotable sentence on a subject, recall might not be as important.

Precision is the percentage or ratio of the units returned that actually meet your query. When you see that first screen of ten search results, if eight of them are really something you are interested in, then you have 80% precision.

The information technology societies once focused on precision and recall. Now their interest has shifted to usability studies and other things. If you look at the literature from the early 1990s back to the mid-1980s, you'll find many articles about precision and recall. There have been far fewer publications recently on these topics.

In those days, when we talked about precision and recall, it seemed the popular consensus was that relevance was the confidence rating. Then Google came along and everyone said, "What about the relevance?" Some people would say that relevance is a canard, that it doesn't mean anything. However, Google's appearance on the scene has changed that perception, and now the community is looking for relevance. Some people would say that relevance is a result of precision of recall. The search results that had both high precision and high recall are the ones that are really relevant to you. Relevance is now measured in many different ways, but not with an algorithm for precision of recall. There are some widely accepted formulas for relevance, recall, and precision. These are the traditional definitions of recall, precision, and relevance, held by the ASIS&T community.

The formulas

Recall = (Number of relevant items retrieved) / (Number of relevant items in the collection)

Precision = (Number of relevant items retrieved) / (Number of items retrieved)

Relevance=(Germane (Precision)) / (Pertinent (Recall))

In measuring relevance, there are many different algorithms that have been used to come up with an answer presented as a percentage. A lot of discussion has been held on relevance but, in the end, it is our confidence in how well we think a particular answer to the query meets your needs.

3.8.2   SEARCH SPEED

In measuring how well search works, we also talk about query processing. In particular, we are interested in how fast the results are returned. There are two parts to that. One part is the query. I've entered a query; now, how fast is the system going to come back to me with an answer? That often depends on how much of that query is going to be held in cache memory and how much is going to be accessed through a hard drive of some kind.

The second part is the results processing. How fast can I see my results? How fast are they returned to the user? Perhaps a message shows that I got 55 hits; I want to see them. I want to click on something and get the actual documents presented to me. That is the display processing. Most systems do not assemble the entire record on the fly, or as you ask for it, from all the different pieces. They have a display server that will show you the results as you indicate your approval by clicking the URL or the path that will take you to the full document. The easy way is just to store the full document somewhere out there and let you retrieve it. In a system like Google, you will be going to the original webpage or whatever is referenced in the URL link.

There are many possible refinements. How long does it take you to narrow down your search? Can you do a search within a search, also known as a recursive search? You have a general set of results. Can you keep that set, discard the unwanted items, and narrow in on precisely what you want, or do you have to start the search over with more or different words so that you can get an answer that is satisfying?

3.8.3   SEARCH USABILITY

Usability is another way that we measure search results to see how good the search system is. This is when we say, "This was really easy to use," "It was very user-friendly," or, "I like the user interface." Qualitative user experience considerations are substantial for the end user, but may not be particularly important to the IT group members who are focused on the quantitative factors leading to the result. When you come to the customer service and user experience interface, you will want their encounter with the system to be a good one. Dr. David Travis has written an excellent checklist of things to consider in search usability; it is available at http://www.userfocus.co.uk/resources/searchchecklist.html.

3.9   KINDS OF SEARCH

Search can be divided into three main kinds—Boolean, browse, and statistical—each of which is accomplished in different ways.

Boolean search is usually behind the little search box on a webpage. You type a word in and get a page with results showing all the articles tagged with that word. If a taxonomy is implemented and the search software will explode the query to include all synonyms, then you will also get all the articles on the same concept but differently stated—that is, the synonyms are also applied to the query. Boolean search often depends on field-formatted data. When data is kept in a database, it is in a field or an element. Field formatted data just means that each part of the data has been tagged or fielded to indicate which field or element this piece of text belongs in. This may be in XML, object oriented, or in a relational database.

Browse uses a navigation tree, either as breadcrumb trails or as a hierarchy. Breadcrumb trails are the listing you frequently see exposing the hierarchy in a website, for example:

United States -. New Mexico -. Bernalillo Country -> Albuquerque

These may be "hardwired" into the user interface or dynamic. Normally it is hardwired, and programmers may be reluctant to take the time and effort to change it. This is a problem, because the logical relationships among the concepts represented are constantly rearranging themselves based on the trends and fads in the science—or other kind of subject area—presented. However, rearrangement can be done dynamically, using the hierarchical view of a taxonomy or thesaurus. Take a look at the taxonomy in the search display for www.MediaSleuth.com. When you click on a term in the left side taxonomic view, it will search for all documents tagged with that taxonomy term in the full underlying database collection of articles. You can choose to see only the items tagged with that term, or all the items underneath that term in the hierarchy as well as that term. It allows for a "roll up" or dive down into the data.

Statistical approaches to search are many, and occupy the bulk of government-funded university research. The techniques go by such names as neural networks [56], latent semantics [57], vector search, Bayesian, co-occurrence, and clustering. The algorithms sound fabulous in the demonstration data sets. They are computationally intensive, and perform much better with well-tagged data. They do depend on Boolean operators for the base inverted indexes but add a great deal of calculation to the results, allowing different views and clusters of the data based on n-grams [58] (sequences of items such as words, syllables, phonemes, and so forth) and data points. These approaches are great for small, deeply mined static sets. If the data is always being added to, updated, or changed in some way, the vectors have to be reset for each analysis, increasing the processing overhead and slowing the reports from the data.

There are search systems that are available on the market and advertised as keyword search, Bayesian systems, Boolean systems, and systems that are primarily ranking algorithms. Here are some examples:

- Keyword

  - HP Autonomy

  - Verity

- Bayesian

  - FAST

  - Lucene

- Boolean

  - Dialog

  - Endeca

- Ranking algorithms

  ○ Google

3.10   THE FAMOUS THEORETICIANS AND THEIR THEORIES ON SEARCH

The theories behind the different kinds of search are based on the work and theories of four famous people.

3.10.1   GEORGE BOOLE AND BOOLEAN ALGEBRA

The first of these theorists was George Boole [59], an English mathematician and logician who lived from 1815 to 1864.

Figure 3.8: George Boole (1815–1864) was an English mathematician and logician. He developed Boolean algebra, the famous and widely used algebraic system of logic.

This is the man behind Boolean algebra, the famous algebraic system of logic, which eventually led to the advent of the digital computer searching we use today. Boolean algebra is the basis of Boolean search, in which webpages are handled as elements of Boolean sets. For our purposes in this chapter, Boolean representation is done by the Venn diagram, which shows the intersection of the two terms in a search. The terms indicated are A and B. we use the Boolean operators AND, OR, and NOT.

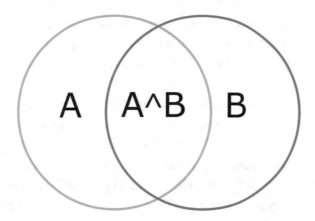

Figure 3.9: A simple Venn diagram illustrates a few of the basic principles of Boolean algebra.

A search for Term A OR Term B would return all the data in both the A and B circles in the diagram. Conversely, Term A AND Term B would be the intersection of the two circles, since the search result must include both terms in order to be an appropriate answer. A NOT B would carve out the B part of the circle and provide a smaller result than A search alone would provide.

3.10.2   THOMAS BAYES AND BAYES' THEOREM

The next theorist of interest is Thomas Bayes, also an English mathematician—and Presbyterian minister—who lived from 1702 to 1761.

Figure 3.10: Thomas Bayes (1702–1761) was an English mathematician who developed Bayes' Theorem.

Bayes' theorem [60] uses probability inductively. He established a mathematical basis for probability inference. The theorem provides a way of calculating the probability that an event will occur in the future, based on the number of times it has occurred in the past.

Bayes theorized that if we have a known set and we know that certain things usually happen in relation to that set, then when we get a new set, we could infer that certain things will happen. In other words, the probability is based on what has happened in the past, so we can forecast what is likely to happen in the future.

It's a nice and fairly well-established algorithm and can be used so that we can say, "Well, if these 5,000 articles were about this, then, if the same term set is used in the next 5,000 articles, probably they are about the same thing." But the distribution of probabilities changes, particularly in active areas such as news or cutting edge science. People might not want to depend on the distribution of historical data to predict future data. A user might also make a new kind of request—something that has not been queried of the system in the past. To get that kind of information out of the network is much harder. We have a computational linguistic difficulty if we explore a set of data with an unknown or new kind of request.

What we have to do is to say, "We knew this to be true in the past and therefore it will be true in the future." You might be looking at terrorist literature, for example, and trying to figure out what may happen in the future, based on what has happened in the past. However, it's entirely possible that some terrorists would be aware of that and that they would be constantly changing, in new and novel ways, so that they could trick the system—figure out the distribution of probabilities and actually give erroneous results to people.

If you depend on a Bayesian engine to keep track of rapidly happening events, you often find that you come up a little off from what actually happens. You have to assume that the prior knowledge is always reliable and indeed represents what will happen in the future, because if you say that it's going to be different, then the next results will be invalid. You want to be sure that the statistical distribution that you come up with to use for modeling your data is consistent.

If you have a consistent set of data inside and it's not going to change much, then the Bayesian approach is a good way to go. Otherwise, you have to constantly train and re-train the data every time you add new data sets, particularly if the direction of the field has changed. While Bayesian methods have value, they need to be used with caution.

Bayesian Cautions

- A user might wish to change the distribution of probabilities.

- A user might make a novel request for information in a previously unanticipated way.

- Computational difficulty is involved in exploring a previously unknown set of data. It will need to be trained for each new set of data and each time a new term is added to the taxonomy.

- Results are dependent on the quality and extent of the prior beliefs used in Bayesian inference processing. That is, a Bayesian network is only as useful as the prior knowledge is reliable.

- An optimistic or pessimistic expectation of the quality of the prior beliefs used in Bayesian inference processing will distort the entire network and invalidate the results.

- The user must ensure the selection of the statistical distribution induced in modeling the data.

- The user must have the proper distribution model to describe the data.

- You have to constantly train and retrain the data.

- You are never free of the data-processing aspects of the system.

3.10.3   OTHER RECENT THEORIES IN SEARCH

Bayesian and Boolean methods are widely used and applied in search. However, the frontiers of search continue to evolve with new theories and applications. Peter Turney and Marco Dorigo are more recent theorists whose findings have been applied to search and data mining.

3.10.4   PETER D. TURNEY AND TURNEY'S ALGORITHM

Our next person of interest is Peter D. Turney [61], a Canadian expert in computational linguistics. One of his main contributions to search technology is Turney's algorithm, which is useful for sentiment analysis [62], the intent behind the words.

Figure 3.11: Peter D. Turney is a Canadian expert in computational linguistics; www.apperceptual.com.

Following is Turney's algorithm for the sentiment analysis of text:

$$\frac{\text{Log2(hits(word and ``excellent'' )hits (poor))}}{\text{(hits(word and ``poor'')hits (excellent)))}}$$

Turney's formula provides the basis for the learning algorithms used in key phrase extraction. They can give you an idea of how you can do just plain extractions of data from a system versus trying to generate terms and even sentiment from the words that are in the source text. Using either Turney's GenEx Algorithm [63] (which uses human input) or the Tree Induction Algorithm [64], he could plot 80% accuracy in the results, which is better than the typical 60% or so from traditional Bayesian inference approaches.

3.10.5 MARCO DORIGO AND ANT COLONY OPTIMIZATION

Marco Dorigo [65] is a Belgian researcher and the initial developer of the ant colony optimization algorithms [66]. He is the research director for the Belgian Fonds de la Recherche Scientifique [67] and co-director of the IRIDIA lab at the Université Libre de Bruxelles [68].

Figure 3.12: Marco Dorigo is a Belgian researcher and the initial developer of the ant colony optimization algorithms.

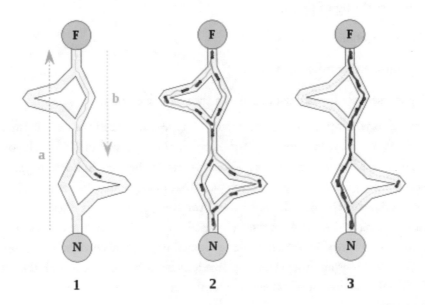

Figure 3.13: A diagram depicting ant colony optimization; http://es.wikipedia.org/wiki/Algoritmo_de_la_colonia_de_hormigas#mediaviewer/File:Aco_branches.svg.

Dorigo's studies are useful in predictive search. Based on what people have asked for in the past, you can predict what they will want in the future. This can be very useful in profiling users and providing a more relevant search result. His research was based on ant colony optimization, part of the field of swarm intelligence [69]. "Swarm Intelligence (SI) is the property of a system whereby the collective behaviors of (unsophisticated) agents interacting locally with their environment cause coherent functional global patterns to emerge" [70].

Dorigo's work makes statements about value importance versus heuristic importance [71], and is therefore useful in search prediction. For example, you might look at the way people are analyzing Twitter feeds in terms of ant colony optimization or swarm intelligence. Frequently, a Twitter stream emerges, seemingly out of nowhere, and it gathers importance very, very quickly, just like a bunch of ants appearing suddenly and attacking a piece of peanut butter and jelly sandwich that landed on the ground only minutes ago.

3.11   OTHER SEARCH APPROACHES

3.11.1   RANKING ALGORITHMS

Finally, we'll take a look at a search approach with a more corporate background: the ranking algorithms of Google. The hallmarks of Google search include the following:

- complex weighting of terms;

- use of term frequency;

- wholly automatic rank output; and,

- ability to use well-formed data such as a thesaurus hierarchy.

The terms that you input—the queries that you type—are called the term inputs. Those term inputs are weighted based on an extremely large number of factors within Google. If you were to get the Google Search of Science to run your in-house searches, they would be using exactly the same algorithms as the www.google.com web search page that is so popular. When you subscribe to the system, Google updates their algorithms for your profile as you search. It tracks to the URL of the computer you are using to improve your search based on what you have asked for or searched for in the past. The real power of its search-ranking algorithms depends on having a huge number of records to vet your rankings against. Most organizations never begin to approach the breadth of the Google database holdings, and it is that sheer volume that makes their algorithms so extraordinarily predictive and persuasive.

This kind of search might work well for you, but if you feel that there are too many false drops (also known as noise, discussed earlier) in Google searches, you are going to get the same situation if you implement it in your own organization. One of the ways you can mitigate that is with the data that you load to Google. You can make it partially well-formed by adding taxonomy terms to it, and then your search improves. Some people have just thrown up their hands because—"Oh no! This is giving me a Google search appliance. I don't know why I ever bothered to do a taxonomy in the first place." However, if you add those terms at the time that you are loading the data to Google, you can search the taxonomy and improve your search results.

3.11.2 NATURAL LANGUAGE PROCESSING IN SEARCH

Another approach used in search, and compatible with the statistical approaches, is natural language processing (NLP [72]), which was briefly discussed earlier. NLP uses natural human language input, or output, or both, in combination with computer processing. Natural language processing is frequently used in conjunction with another system. There are certain basic approaches in natural language processing.

- Syntactics: the rules for the language and how they govern the sentences in any individual language [73].

- Semantics: the words themselves and how they are stated and behave [74].

- Morphology of those words: the smallest meaningful elements in words, such as plural endings [75].

- Phrase logical implementations: the use of those words in phrases.

- Stemming, or lemmatization[76]: cutting off the endings, such as the "eds," and the "ings," and other suffixes attached to the word root.

- Statistical options: as outlined above.

- Grammatical applications, some of them involving full graphing of sentences: if you remember graphing sentences from school, computers do a similar thing in NLP.

Then, at the end of the day there is plain common sense. It's really handy to have common-sense algorithms that non-programmers can develop, based on their knowledge of the language and the subject matter. That is often done in an indexing rule base. Natural language processing utilizing Boolean operators, for example, makes for a nice rule-based system.

All of these approaches are used, to some extent and to varying degrees, in search software. Some software uses NLP as a base layer and never lets anyone touch it. Some software uses NLP as an interface for people. Often, NLP approaches involve "black box" applications that are invisible to the users, because the algorithms, particularly the grammatical ones, are hard to follow, and programmers don't want to allow users direct access in case those users make changes that are detrimental to the application. These "black box" applications are losing popularity since they are hard for the users to understand and to work with to improve their own search experience.

3.11.3 AUTOMATIC LANGUAGE PROCESSING

What has become more popular is automatic language processing (ALP), which includes the following components.

- Automatic translation

- Automatic indexing

- Automatic abstracting

- Artificial intelligence

- Searching

- Spell checking

- Spam filtering

- Natural language processing

- Computational linguistics

I used to attend many conferences about computational linguistics, artificial intelligence, and automatic translation meetings. I also usually attend the ASIS&T [77] meetings, which focus more on the information science realm. Suddenly, many people that I saw at the artificial intelligence meetings were showing up at the ASIS&T meetings. There is a lot of overlap in these fields, but modern ALP is trying to automate most of the pieces. It's essentially NLP with a few more computational heuristics, and it lends itself well to search.

3.11.4 STATISTICAL SEARCH

The components of statistical search are as follows.

Cluster analysis [78]

Neural networks [79]

Co-occurrence [80]

Bayesian inference [81]

Latent semantic indexing [82]

Statistical search is primarily Bayesian. It has different levels of usage of the Bayesian algorithms. You might hear about the work of Gerald Salton and his "smart factors" from Cornell, or "cluster analysis" from other sources; you might hear about neural nets and neural networks from concept analysts; you might hear about co-occurrence engines from HP Autonomy; or you might hear about Bayesian inference engines from other people. They're all doing a variation on the same theme. They are all doing heavy statistical analysis of the data and trying using some of the ALP or NLP techniques—to provide an excellent search result for you.

3.12 INVERTED FILES, PARSING, DISCOVERY, AND CLUSTERING

All of the different kinds of searches listed in Section 3.12 have in common inverted files and Boolean logic. We'll cover inverted files in the next section. Inverted files and Boolean logic are basic to most or all search. The use of parsing methodologies, discovery presentations, and clustering algorithms further enhances the options available.

3.12.1 THE INVERTED INDEX

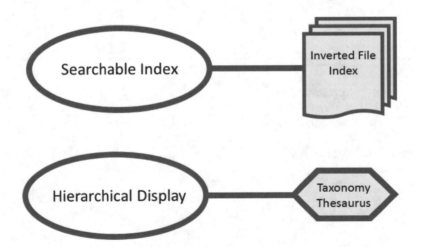

Figure 3.14: The relationship between an inverted file index and a taxonomy or thesaurus.

Earlier, we briefly mentioned inverted indexes—the alphabetical list of all the terms in your taxonomy and the information about where they come from within the hierarchy. A way to combine that inverted file—the index that is searchable by the computer—and the hierarchical display of your taxonomy—is the key to search systems. Here's an example of some text that we want to search.

Outline of Presentation

1. Define key terminology

2. Thesaurus tools

   a. Features

   b. Functions

3. Costs

   a. Thesaurus construction

   b. Thesaurus tools

4. Why & when?

Pretend that this outline is a webpage and focus on any one term, like "thesaurus." To build an inverted file of this data, we would make an alphabetic list, and it would look like this:

Simple Inverted File Index

&	key
1	of
2	outline
3	presentation
4	terminology
construction	thesaurus
costs	tools
define	when
features	why
functions	

If we wanted to make it more complex, we would add stop words and some conditions:

Complex Inverted File Index

& - Stop	Key—L2, P2, H
1 - Stop	of - Stop
2 - Stop	outline—L1, P1, T

3 - Stop	presentation—L1, P3, T
4 - Stop	terminology—L2, P3, H
construction—L7, P2, SH	thesaurus (1)—L3, P1, H
	(2)—L7, P1, SH
	(3)—L8, P1, SH
costs—L6, P1, H	tools (1)—L3, P2, H
	(2)—L8, P2, SH
define—L2, P1, H	when—L9, P3, H
features—L4, P1, SH	why—L9, P1, H
functions—L5, P1, SH	

"L" = Line number or place in the source listing

"P" = paragraph break

"SH" = subject heading or term

The example above shows where each term appears in my taxonomy hierarchy. This gives me and my computer a way to combine the terms, because I know from their positions where they are located within the hierarchy. At the end of the day, this is what a complex inverted index display looks like, and it is basic to search function.

3.12.2 PARSING

Parsing is a computer operation that indicates the place we break a term or term phrase in text. For example, consider a valid term from a taxonomy, "Aeronautical engineering." For it to be specific, we need to have both words considered as a single unit. Otherwise it is engineering and aeronautical, which would provide a different search result. Used together they have a special meaning. We therefore would want to keep them together in the search. To accomplish this, we add an indicator as to where we would like the computer to parse the words so we can keep the meaning where it is important. Setting of the parsing rules is an important part of the database search system specification and creation.

3.12.3   OTHER SEARCH TECHNIQUES

We use techniques such as stemming, truncation, and wildcards to do search. In addition, we accommodate all those misspellings, variant spellings, and so forth, so that we can make search even better by using some of the following options.

- Word and Term Parsing Techniques

    ○ Stemming—Lemmatization—removing suffixes so that only the root word is left

        • -ing, -ed, -es, -'s, -s', etc.

    ○ Depluralization—making something singular

        • Cars → Car

    ○ Truncation—shortening by cutting off

        • On the right side this is easy, you just chop the stem

            - Unexpectedly → Unexpected

        • On the left side this is more difficult because it builds a full secondary index

            - Unexpectedly → Expectedly

    ○ Wildcards—usually an asterisk "*" that may be substituted for any of a defined subset of all possible characters [83]

        • Organi*ation will cover both Organization and Organisation

    ○ Variant Spellings

        • Center, Centre

    ○ Hyphens bind words in search. Without a space, the parsing algorithm has no way to know where to break the phrase. Therefore the hyphenated word is searchable only exactly as it is presented in the test. The second half of the word disappears into the computer ether and is not searchable or findable. Avoid hyphens whenever possible. Your users will not know that they should add them in their search string.

    ○ The use of wildcards and some stemming techniques is very common, as is right truncation. Left truncation is difficult, because the first letter has changed, and because the inverted index is alphabetical, you have to build an entire new inverted file. This can make for an extremely large index very quickly. Using wildcards instead might be another option, since left truncation is very expensive to implement. Before you do any left truncation, examine what it is going to do to your system.

3.12.4 DISCOVERY SEARCH OPTIONS

Discovery search has received a great deal of research monies and a great deal of attention recently. Discovery search "...engines are helpful when you're not quite sure what you're looking for, or aren't looking at all. They help you uncover information you didn't know existed, didn't know you needed, or didn't know you wanted—yet delights you when you find it" [84]. Some recent studies have shown, however, that only about 2% of searchers' time is actually spent in discovery, while 98% of their time is spent doing whatever search is needed to update their knowledge. That is, the searcher spends 98% of their time looking for a known or suspected item, not looking for new and serendipitous items.

Some of the big questions in search are "What kind of search are you or your users going to do? Are you doing discovery—looking for new things and new ways of combining things? Or are you trying to do an exhaustive everything search? Do you need relevance, recall, and precision, or are you in discovery mode?" The answers to these questions will make a big difference in what kind of search implementation you design.

3.12.5 CLUSTERING

Yippy [85] (formerly Clusty) is a discovery search engine developed by Vivisimo and sold to Yippy, Inc. It is very useful for discovery and looking at data in new ways. It searches on the fly and does automatic document clustering, but in my experience it doesn't return the same clusters—or results—each time, even if the search query is the same. This may anger some researchers who prefer additive results; that is, they want to see everything that the search returned before plus anything that is new.

In clustering search results, you can group everything together into hierarchical clusters, or you can partition information resources. Even in a cluster application, you can add a thesaurus, although the clustering algorithm will recluster or reorder the information each time a search is executed. Any work you have put into creating a hierarchical taxonomy will disappear in a clustering algorithm. The search will be improved, since the data is consistently tagged, but the presentation will change with each update of the database. One can accomplish clustering in many different ways that are beyond the scope of this text, except to make you aware that they exist.

- Distance measure [86]

- Hierarchical [87] clustering using either agglomerative hierarchical clustering [88] or basic concept clustering [89]

- Partitional clustering [90] or separating the data into separate bins, buckets, or partitions based on a set criteria using mathematical k-means and derivatives, k-means clustering [91], fuzzy *c*-means clustering [92], or quality threshold (QT) clustering [93]

- Locality sensitive hashing [94]

- Graph theoretic methods [95]

- Spectral clustering [96]

3.13   FACETED SEARCH

In faceted search, the subject metadata has been put into different fields or elements and is maintained from different authority files or pick lists to populate those fields. Facets are sort systems along the lines of post-coordinated search refinements. They allow another way to filter the data for the user. If you are shopping for a men's shirt, size XL long sleeved in flannel, faceted search is a perfect way to find the item.

When a search query is created, the search software is directed to look at a user-defined combination of any set of the facets—including the subject metadata or conceptual thesaurus facet—to execute the query in the database. On a consumer site that sells clothing, for example, the user can search by size, type of garment, color, or price as individual facets.

Faceted search is broadly applied in consumer shopping websites. Most of our readers will have used them on L.L.Bean or Target or Amazon websites. The Endeca Search software particularly embraces faceted searching. To implement it, you may need to build several small facets or taxonomies—one to support each of the individual facets you allow as searchable fields. Sometimes the individual branches of taxonomies are built as facets. The relationships between the terms supported by the hierarchical and associative relationships allow for cross-field referencing if the implementing software will support it.

In explaining what facets are, Heather Hedden has commented on their usefulness in commerce:

> *"You can remember what a facet is by thinking of "face," as in a multi-faceted diamond. Other names for facet include dimension, aspect, or attribute. It could be the set of characteristics that describe a product (category, size, color, price, intended user, etc.), an image (thing, persons, location, occasion, etc.), or a document (document type, topic, author, source, etc.) In a business or enterprise taxonomy, facets for content management may include content type, product or service line, department or function, and topic. Named entities, such as person names, company names,*

agency names, and names of laws might also each be a facet. Facets allow users to limit, restrict, or filter results by chosen criteria, one from each facet" [97].

Dr. Ranganathan's principles are still widely applied and popular in the search world, especially in e-commerce. The Endeca faceted search module is popular with online marketers, because they want to offer many different ways to filter data.

Figure 3.15: Sample of facted search. http://blog.thanxmedia.com/blog/wp-content/uploads/2010/08/Gander.jpg via Google image search.

In the case of Endeca, their biggest usages are in retail ecommerce. In general, users who are ordering products online are going to be using an Endeca search system. For example, as shown in the image above, there is a shirt that comes in five colors and four sizes. Perhaps it has some additional attributes to it. The shopper wants to search on any one of those classifications and get the same shirt.

As a searcher on this site, let's say I want my blouse in a women's size X, and my husband wants his shirt in a men's size Y. He wants blue while I prefer green. You can create those orders with the same general properties. The shirt classification has a lot of sub-facets to it. The system is searching all of those different facets, which we know more familiarly as size and shape and color, and complete the order. Behind the scenes we aren't using one single taxonomic list but rather several sub-lists that identify those objects.

In constructing the taxonomy, you could have built each of those sub-lists out as a separate branch. More likely, you would build them all as separate little taxonomies, because they are basically authority lists or pick lists. Any one of them is consistent. If I want women's clothing on L.L.Bean, I am going to click on Women's Clothing, and then the website is going to tell me that it has pants, shirts, and other things, and I can choose from those. Those are facets in this search system, and I can click through them and get increasingly more detailed information.

In Lucene [98], which is an open source search system, I can do the same thing but a bit differently. Here the facets are giving me an individual item. There can be many different facets, so I am able to search for a manufacturer from a drop-down list of manufacturers. Using a different example, here, I am wanting to purchase a new camera. On an electronics website, I hope that in addition to choosing from a drop-down list of manufacturers, I can narrow my options by price, resolution, or zoom range. Choosing an item from each of these categories—or drop-down lists, or facets—narrows my search.

Once again, I hope you can see the influence of Boolean logic in this search example. My query could be thought of as looking something like this:

Manufacturer = Canon AND Price = $500 - $800 AND Zoom = 16x

…and will result in finding a Canon camera for $600 with a 16 X zoom lens.

3.14   THE POSSIBILITIES OF SEARCH INTERFACES

As a user, wouldn't it be fabulous if you could have the system read your mind and instantly offer the topic you're searching for in a list of suggestions? Actually, we've already seen that enhancement and it's rather impressive—at least when what you're looking for is there. The profiling and heuristics we discussed about plus your own search history enable a search software to "read your mind" and provide the items you would be most interested in. What if those suggestions not only returned a comprehensive and relevant set of articles, but also offered other tools to assist in your research?

How about suggestions to broaden your search with topics related to the query you entered? Or suggestions of more specific examples of your query, some of which you may not have been aware of? What if the search returns page included recent blog, forum, or video postings, case studies, product descriptions, webinars, and news items? What about the offer of an expanded search to include a select group of sites of professional organizations, publishers, consultants, or specialized wikis that would include more items tagged with your search query words? Would it help to see from where in the world the latest work has been published? Whether there is an upcoming conference that includes presentations about it? Notes from a panel discussion or presentation held recently? Perhaps you'd like a list of authors who have written about that topic? Or a list of others inside or outside your organization whose project includes your search query topic as a component?

It's all possible, and there are already examples of many of these search enhancements, but not all, and perhaps not in the useful combinations envisioned in your dreams.

Basic requirements for implementing these enhancements—and for the semantic web that it naturally leads to—are a taxonomy of query terms (or several taxonomies mapped to each other), a good automatic categorization engine, some agreement about what metadata to capture and how to store it, and a little coding magic—most of which must still be custom coded. Many of those enhancements would make users much more productive and efficient, cutting down on wasted time and duplication and opening up exciting new possibilities—but those systems don't quite exist just yet.

The information science community can look forward to search interface advances—content management and portal systems that build in the tools for delivering such search enhancements, working toward standards that make integration and use of content assets easier, letting our imaginations conjure up ways to harness the power of information. In the meantime, let's move on to a discussion of search in web applications.

CHAPTER 4

Implementing a Taxonomy in a Database or on a Website

The workings of a taxonomy or thesaurus in a database or website can seem mysterious. Some of the following information is a review of what we have covered in previous chapters, and I believe it bears repeating here.

Let's take a look at how things work behind the scenes.

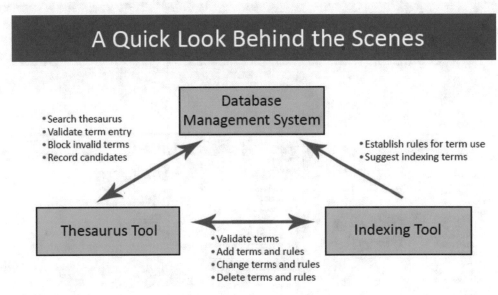

Figure 4.1: A quick look behind the scenes showing the connections among the various parts of a database system that includes taxonomy and indexing features.

4.1 START FROM THE BEGINNING

Looking at the above figure, we have a Thesaurus Tool, an Indexing Tool, and a Database Management System. All three of them work together. The Thesaurus Tool communicates with the Indexing Tool in term and rule addition, term validation, and changing and deleting terms and rules. When we perform one of these functions in the Thesaurus Tool, the Indexing Tool needs to be aware of the changes so that it will provide updated terms for the records in the Database Management System. When the Thesaurus Tool interacts with the Database Management System, some of the functions might be to search the thesaurus, validate term entry against records, record candidate terms for possible future addition to the thesaurus, and block terms that are invalid or not in the thesaurus. The Indexing Tool provides information to the Database Management System, establishing rules or conditions for when terms should be applied, and suggesting those terms where appropriate—by pulling them from the Thesaurus Tool.

4.1.1   THE TAXONOMY OR THESAURUS TOOL

In order to create this system, we need the taxonomy or thesaurus in digital form, either as a separate file or as it exists in a specialized software application. The figure below is a screenshot from the editorial user interface of a thesaurus software application.

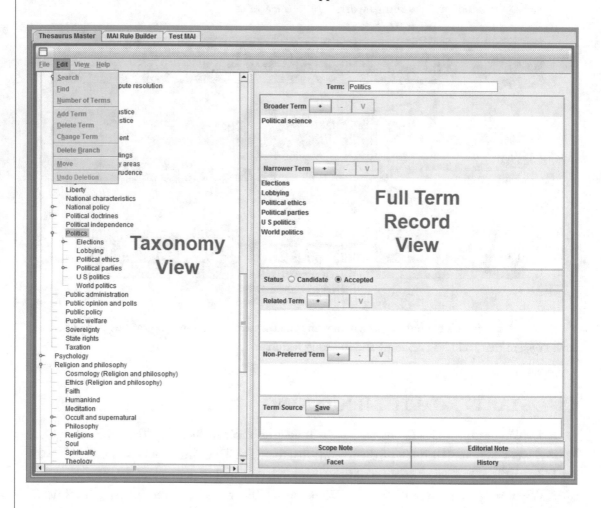

Figure 4.2: Viewing a thesaurus from the editorial interface of the Data Harmony Thesaurus Master software application.

The left panel shows a taxonomy view from the hierarchical viewpoint. The right panel shows a term record. The broader terms, the narrower terms, status, related terms, and other term record fields (synonyms, history, scope notes, and so forth) are displayed in the right panel. A large amount of information is stored as an object associated with each term. The highlighted term in the left panel is *Politics*. The links between this term and the other terms in the thesaurus hierarchy, including a broader term—*Political science*—and six narrower terms that are displayed in the right panel, are also part of the "object."

4.1.2   THE INDEXING TOOL

Next, we need an Indexing Tool to work with the Thesaurus Tool. Indexing, the act of actually adding or linking the taxonomy terms to the content itself, is what makes all our work worthwhile. It can be a manual, assisted, or fully automatic action. The terms might be added to the properties tables of PDFs; to MS Office documents (Word, Excel, Powerpoint); to the metadata for the images; to the Meta Name Keyword header in an HTML page; to the proper table in a relational database; to a field in a database export format; or to the appropriate element in an XML file. Wherever that taxonomy term (tag, or index term) is to be placed, some computer assistance to ensure that the full breadth and depth of the taxonomy is used is shown to the editor/indexer for selection or applied directly to the text. The screenshot below shows a data entry screen. When the data is entered, a popup screen of potential taxonomy terms to choose from is presented. The consuming application or data repository needs to have a place to put these terms.

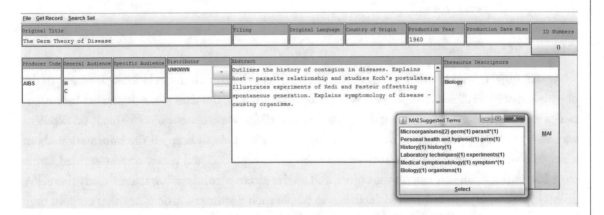

Figure 4.3: View of Data Harmony software with a pop-up window showing suggested terms from the M.A.I. automated indexing.

4.1.3   THE DATABASE MANAGEMENT SYSTEM

Next, we need the Database Management Tool and some associated search software. Database management systems (DBMSs), relational database management systems (RDBMS), and content management systems (CMSs) are widely available, and there are dozens of them available, from simple freeware and shareware options to customized programs by software giants like Oracle.

There are two basic kinds of database management approaches—*relational databases* and *object-oriented databases*.

Relational Databases

In relational databases, information is organized into a series of tables organized according to a relational model. In a relational model, each table or collection of data is linked to other columns or groups of columns. This creates a system of primary and secondary keys for the database that uniquely identify each column. Using this method, a relationship is established between each bit of data (row) in the table and a row in another table by reaching out to it and listing it as a valid *foreign key*. A foreign key is a column or group of columns in one table that points to the primary key of another table. These relational models offer a wide variety of options and can be refined by creating and recreating the tables, repopulating the data in the rows and creating new relationships between the tables as needed.

Adding taxonomies in relational databases simply involves adding a taxonomy table as one of the columns and then linking it in the overall design, using the keys to the appropriate data for indexing display and search.

Object-Oriented Databases

An object-oriented database is quite differently constructed from a relational database. In the object-oriented database, the "object" is kept together. That is, the data is not separated into many tables and rows, but just created and maintained as individual pieces or objects. This is an excellent way to work with publications or museum objects. You are able to keep all the information about a single object in a single place. It does not need to be exploded and recast or reassembled into a page for editing. You just call up the object, and all the pieces accompanying it are already there. We usually work with object-oriented databases in which each document, article, or other content item is stored as an object. We also frequently use a hybrid approach, storing the content items as objects and taxonomies or term lists in tables like a taxonomic view for easy display, and link the terms back to all the objects, or articles, that have been indexed using that term. Object programming and data are easily and effectively supported by XML.

Apples and Oranges, or Two Kinds of Apples?

Whether you are working with an object-oriented system or a relational database management system (RBDMS), you will need a place for your taxonomy terms to be housed. In object-oriented code it is another XML element; in RDBMS it is another field in a table with rows to accommodate the terms. You want to be sure that the data will transfer over appropriately from where it is stored. Below are two figures that indicate where in the workflow the taxonomy terms are located.

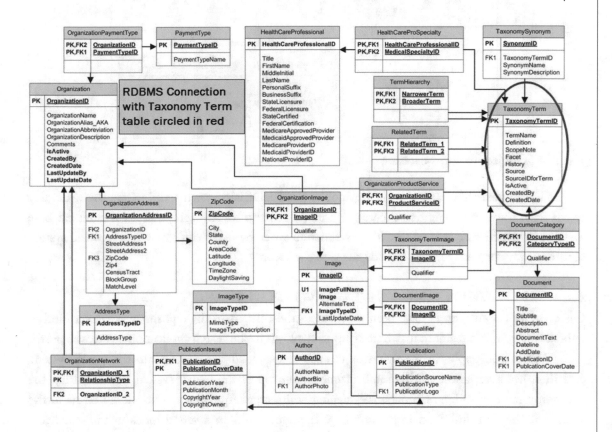

Figure 4.4: RDBMS connection with taxonomy term table circled in red.

Object-Oriented Model

Object 1: Maintenance Report   **Object 1 Instance**

Date		01-12-01
Activity Code		24
Route No.		I-95
Daily Production		2.5
Equipment Hours		6.0
Labor Hours		6.0

Object 2: Maintenance Activity

Activity Code	
Activity Name	
Production Unit	
Average Daily Production Rate	

Figure 4.5: Object-oriented database model.

The figures show examples of both object and RDBMS systems and where the taxonomy terms fit in the implementation process. You might have an XML-based, object-oriented database system, in which case you can build in a function whereby users enter new text and the system automatically suggests terms and adds them to the records.

4.1.4   IMPLEMENTING THE TAXONOMY IN SEARCH

Once the taxonomy terms have been attached to the content in the repository, whatever kind of database system it is resident in, we are ready to deploy it to the search application or the web portal.

When you apply taxonomy terms to each record, load the records into the search system, and then use a variation of that same taxonomy on top of the search system, you are using the taxonomy for two different functions—tagging and search. Applying the taxonomy terms to the records is the first and most important step. Then you build an inverted index of the searchable data, which is presented in the user interfaces through the search function. This data might be just the taxonomy terms, or the title, abstract, and taxonomy terms. With this method, your users will experience better results.

Here's a workflow diagram that might help to clarify things.

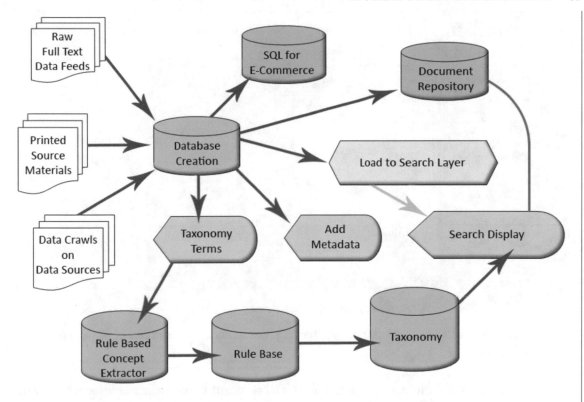

Figure 4.6: Diagram showing how a taxonomy can be integrated into a search system.

You might have a large amount of raw data—records or content items—that you put into a data repository or database management system. You add the taxonomy terms to the records in that repository. The repository could be stored in a search system, and you might or might not use a presentation layer for the search function, or it could be stored as an SQL file for e-commerce. From the repository where you have added the taxonomy terms to the records, you can spin it out to different systems or outputs for different purposes—web search, e-commerce, printed items, webpage navigation, indexes for publications, author tagging, social networking, profiling of artifacts, and so on.

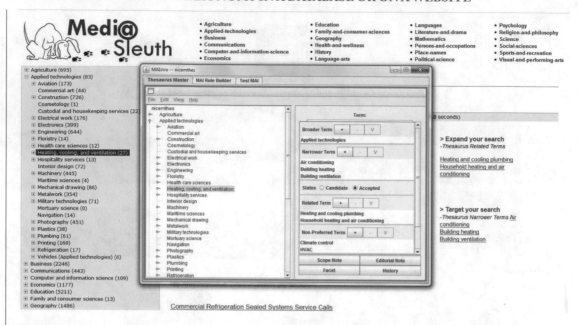

Figure 4.7: A view of www.mediasleuth.com showing how terms in the term record become the terms in the search interface.

In this example, the narrower terms in the term record become the narrower terms in the search interface, and the related terms from the term record will also be posted in the search interface. There is a direct connection between the two.

4.1.5   PUTTING TOGETHER THE PIECES FOR A PHENOMENAL WEBSITE

Now we have our Taxonomy Tool with our taxonomy, our Indexing Tool for tagging our content, our Database Management System for content storage, our Search System to bring it all together, and a Search Presentation Layer for the user interface.

There are a number of ways that we can use our taxonomy to improve a website and the users' experience with that website. The overall goal is to integrate the taxonomy so that your users can more readily find the items tagged with the taxonomy terms, and there are a number of ways to achieve this. Most of them are compatible with each other and can be implemented in combination with each other. Let's look at how the taxonomy terms become connected in a website:

- application of appropriate taxonomy terms to enhance findability of contents in the database;

- browseable categories for a directory of contents in the associated database;

- browseable faceted navigation of the contents in the associated database;

- smart search for term equivalents or synonyms;

- original or modified taxonomy terms as labels for categories; and,

- navigation aids incorporating taxonomy terms and their relationships to help users search, browse, or discover their way to the desired content.

To see some of this in action, go to a website—we use www.accessintegrity.com in this example—and right-click on some non-active region of the page. A menu similar to the pop-up menu shown below should appear.

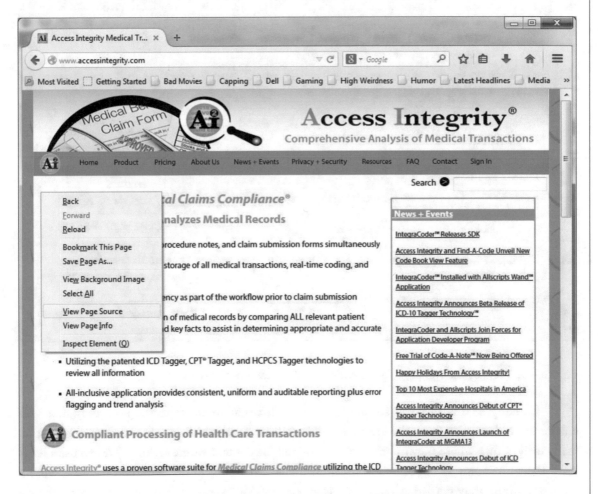

Figure 4.8: Discovering a thesaurus associated with a webpage—"View Page Source" is highlighted in the drop-down menu on the left side of the screen at www.accessintegrity.com.

Clicking on the "View Source" menu item will bring up a page similar to that in the figure below, which displays the source code for the webpage where you can see the meta name="keywords" field. Not all websites will have this field, but many do.

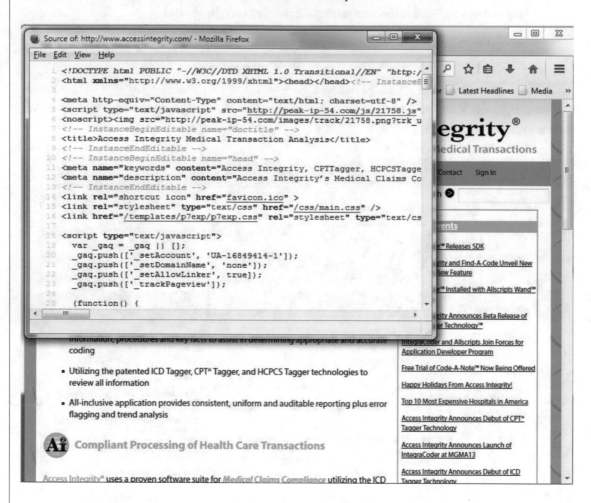

Figure 4.9: View of the webpage source code at www.accessintegrity.com.

Looking at this site, you see the hierarchical list that comes from the taxonomy. This will enable us to determine how the creators of this website organize their content, thereby giving us some insight into where they might have categorized the content we are seeking. We can use a term from their taxonomy as our search query, knowing that the content items in their database will be tagged appropriately with that term. This is an example of "Application of appropriate taxonomy terms to enhance findability of contents in the database" from the list above.

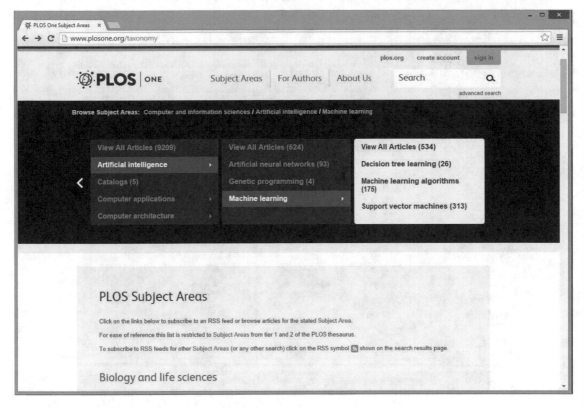

Figure 4.10: An example from PLOS ONE showing browseable categories for a directory of contents in the associated database.

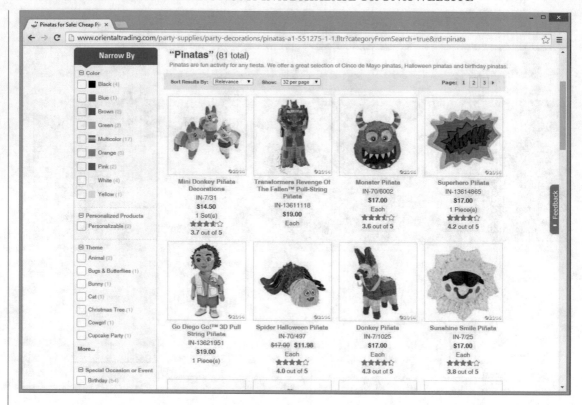

Figure 4.11: An example from Oriental Trading showing browseable faceted navigation of the contents in the associated database.

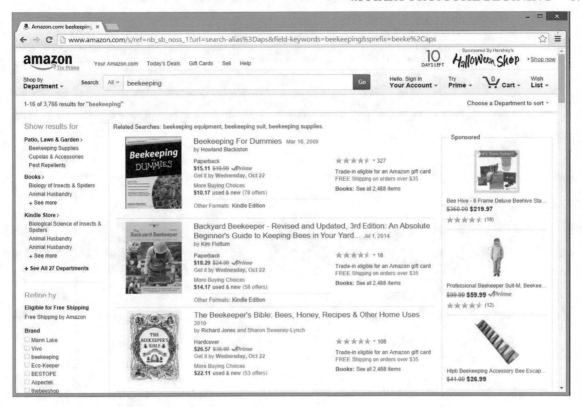

Figure 4.12: An example from Amazon showing browseable faceted navigation of the contents in the associated database.

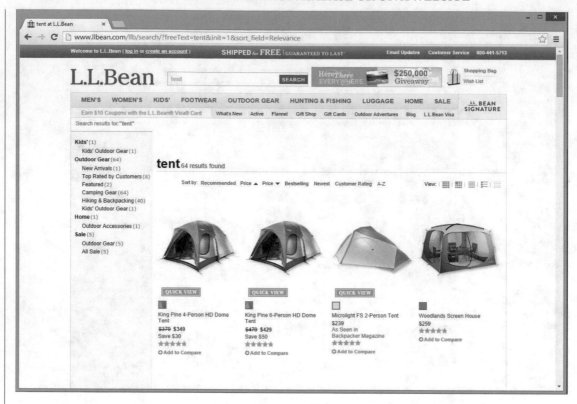

Figure 4.13: An example from L.L. Bean showing browseable faceted navigation of the contents in the associated database.

Figure 4.14: An example from Wikipedia showing smart search for term equivalents.

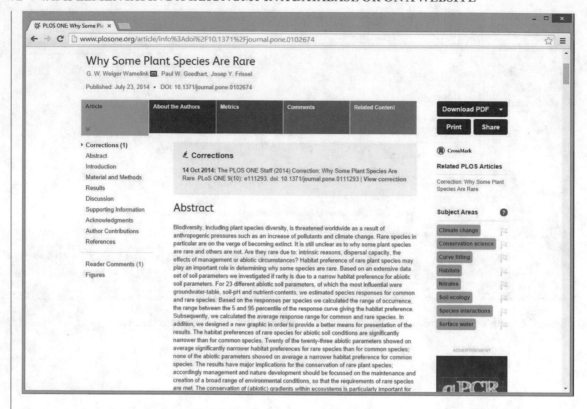

Figure 4.15: An example from PLOS ONE showing taxonomy terms as labels for categories.

Navigation aids incorporating taxonomy terms and their relationships to help users search, browse, or discover their way to the desired content.

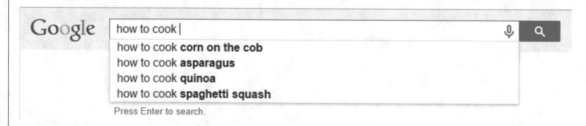

Figure 4.16: An example from GOOGLE autocomplete, this feature is often integrated with taxonomy terms.

Looking at the examples above, you can see how you could use the same set of taxonomy terms many places in your website.

4.2   EMPOWERING THE AUTHORS

As we continue discussing semantic integration and more specifically, use cases, here is a different kind of use case. This case shows the integration of the author submission module into the editorial production workflow. In this case, a potential author is uploading a conference paper to the ASIS&T site. The author or person uploading a paper for consideration fills in the data in a document template, attaching images and graphics as necessary. API calls to the automatic indexing system present a list of suggested indexing terms from the taxonomy to the author for selection. The automatic suggestion of terms is done based on the content submitted by the author.

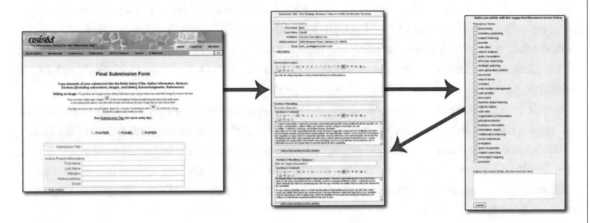

Figure 4.17: An author submission feature connected with a taxonomy allows the author to select their own metadata at the beginning of the publishing pipeline.

The author who is submitting the article can then click on the terms they think are appropriate to their paper. Then the paper is saved, already indexed. This saves time and effort and helps to eliminate confusion all the way through the production system. Since the terms were suggested by the indexing system and selected—essentially approved—by the author, we hope that they are more appropriate terms than might be assigned by the author alone, the taxonomy and indexing system alone, or another person tasked with adding terms after the fact. We have found that, on average, authors choose more keywords for their papers than indexers would.

Behind the scenes in this example, the data can be saved either as HTML or as an XML file so that it can be integrated into the general editorial workflow.

For an author submission system, an author authority file can be built while you build the journal article database. For each upload, the system can create a full author record, including fields for name, address, URLs, websites, telephone numbers, fax number, email, and any other fields that are important in your organization or your workflow. After you have built the authority file, you might allow authors to add further information and verify that what you have is correct. You could even allow them to add a profile about themselves, and perhaps encourage them to claim and add an ORCID (see Book 2, Chapter 2, Section 2.6 (Authority Files)) as well. Combined, these activities result in a taxonomy term profile, also called a semantic fingerprint, for the author—a profile of their activities based on the taxonomy terms associated with them. The word "semantic" is broadly used to describe taxonomy terms, descriptors, keywords, and subject headings, especially when they are applied to textual objects.

As the author authority list grows, and if their physical address or location is included in each author record, you can start to place them geographically and see where there are concentrations of study in various geographical regions and in fields of study. The detection of a highly distributed research staff throughout the nation or throughout the world becomes possible. This taxonomy tagging of people allows you to find people who are working on similar things, because they describe what they are working on using the taxonomy. These connections are solid and go beyond the traditional linking of authors by co-occurrence and co-citation. Now you can link them by their semantic profile in addition to their publication profile.

It is also possible to display coauthor relationships. The radial graph view below shows that an author has published papers in conjunction with the authors in the central area, and that those authors have published in conjunction with the authors in the outer circle. In this example, you have two levels of author linkages. You can do an analysis similar to the one shown below on a given subject as well as on an author name, providing a visual representation of how different subject areas overlap, connect, or merge.

radialgraphview

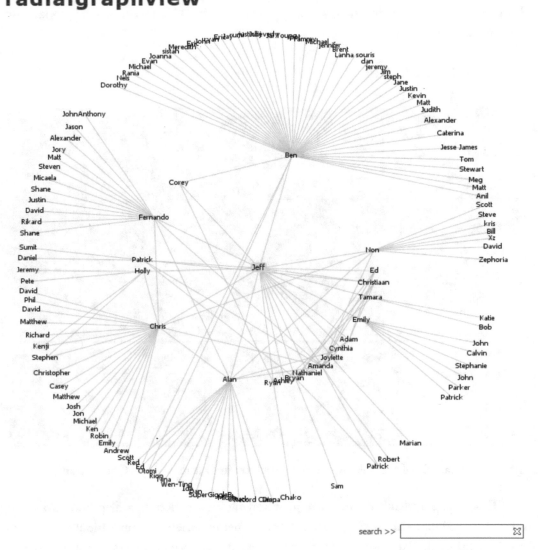

Figure 4.18: A radial graph image produced by Jeffrey Heer and showcased in the perfuse.org gallery.

4.3   MATCHING UP PEOPLE WITH PEOPLE, PLACES, AND SUBJECT AREAS

Based on the same author data we discussed above, and in this case adding a place name or location coupled with its GPS coordinates, we can create a list of authors by location. The markers on the figure below represent clusters of people who have published on a particular topical area, showing communities of practice. Using the author, their subject profile, or semantic fingerprint, and the GPS coordinates of their location, we can see where in the U.S. researchers are working on this topical area.

4.3.1   DATA MASHUPS

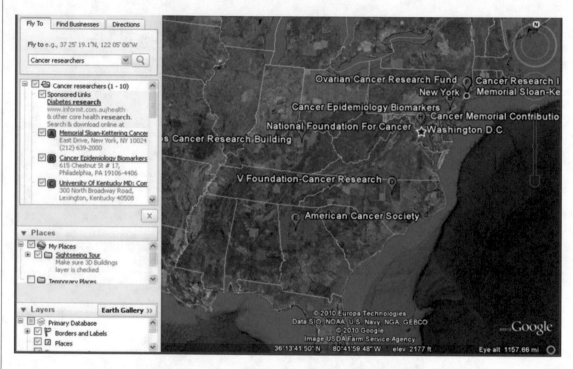

Figure 4.19: Example of the AACR cancer research centers created within Google Earth.

This map is a match-up, or mashup, overlaying information on a map from Google Earth. In this case, we looked at cancer research institutes. Because there are publications that are indexed with the same or similar taxonomy terms from a list of authors with addresses or GPS coordinates, we can use those three information items—terms, author names, and addresses—to produce this graphical display of where they are located. For scientists looking to collaborate on research, it is helpful to know where others doing similar research are located.

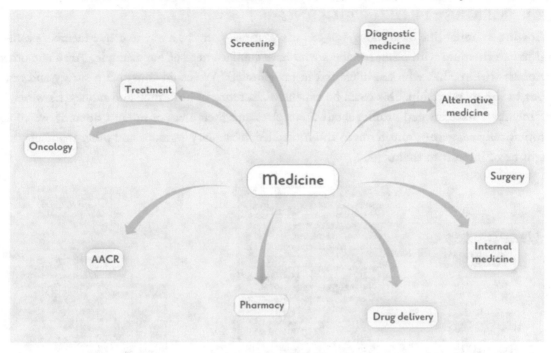

Figure 4.20: Taxonomy display implementation by Bob Kasenchak using SpicyNodes.com software.

Here is another option. This one is using a free program called Spicy Nodes [99]. In my experience it doesn't work well for large taxonomies, but it is really fun for small ones. This shows a term—AACR—and the terms that are the next level down in the hierarchy, based on the broader–narrower term relationships in the AACR taxonomy. Medicine is shown as a major topical area, and then the arrows point to the terms that are on the next level down in the hierarchy. The example above shows the second level, and you can continue to follow terms down through the lower levels of the hierarchy. This is a fun way to display your taxonomy. It also displays connections that you don't normally see in a flat navigation list.

4.3.2   FIND EXPERTS

Another way to use taxonomies is to find and develop a list of experts, perhaps reviewers who journal editors can call on to work on a project or review an article for publication. It can be difficult to locate someone who has the appropriate expertise. The journal editor may have a flat list on paper or in an Excel spreadsheet, but if it were transformed into a dynamic taxonomy, potential reviewers could be found from the semantic profiles, providing them with a map of experts and their respective expertise. The information could also be overlaid on a geographical map for determining physical proximity, or on a subject area map to show whether the expert in question works in the established core of the field or if they are pushing the boundaries of a given research area.

4.3.3   MEMBER PROFILE TAGGING

Following a similar line of thinking, you can use your taxonomy as a way to create member profiles and match them up with other members who have similar interests. For example, "Are there other members within SLA who are interested in taxonomies?" We could construct a survey and send it out to the membership. This could be expensive, in terms of both time and money. However, if the members have created profiles about themselves and their areas of interest or study, we could automatically suggest—from terms in the controlled vocabulary—groups and other members that might be of interest to them.

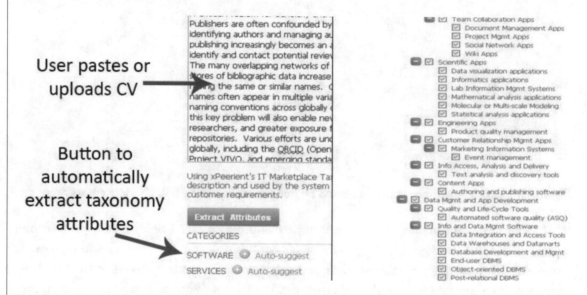

Figure 4.21: Example from the xPeerient taxonomy http://www.xpeerient.com/.

Here's another example. This one is an intriguing system called xPeerient [100]. xPeerient matches up technology sellers with technology buyers. When someone has a bit of information about hardware, software, or a service, they upload it to xPeerient in an online template. Then they click a button to auto-suggest the taxonomy attributes. The attributes that match this profile come up into the listing of terms—on the right—and they click the ones that are appropriate. The system reviews the profiles and finds matches. If one user wants to buy software and another selling, their profiles are matched up, and the two users can conduct their business. It's a bit like an online dating service—for IT hardware and software purchases.

4.4   MUSINGS ON NAME DISAMBIGUATION

On April 19, 2011, the *Wall Street Journal* published an article about the need for customer name authority control in banks. Okay, so maybe that is not what they said, exactly. What they did outline was the issue of Arabic names and the many ways to state them. This creates difficulties for banks and other organizations that try to track the information or put a hold on funds for organizations or individuals. The example used was Moammar Gadhafi. His first name could be transliterated as Muammar, Mummar, Mohamed Mahmut, or Mehmud—or one of more than 20 other variants. The same goes with his last name, which could be Gaddafi, Ghathafi, Elkaddafi, El-Kaddafi, Al-Gaddafi, Gadhafi, Qaddafi, Al-Qadhafi, El-Qaddfi, Qadhafi, Abu Miryar Al-Qahafi, Ghadaffi, and others. Any combination of these names is valid. There are further complications of the Abu or Al or El and other definite articles and designations of honor, making things even more interesting.

The UN Sanctions group lists 12 variations for his name. The UN prefers a single form of the name (Muammar Mohammed Abu Miryar Qahafi), as do the Swiss (Muammar Ghedklafi). However, there is nothing unusual or illegal about someone filing under any of several valid variations of their name.

Arabic does not have a single transliteration standard but rather, a number of them, which causes confusion in resultant naming of groups and consistent application in the West. Kanji characters (Korean, Chinese, and Japanese) or Tamil have fewer broadly used transliterations and therefore more easily understood translations. There are attempts at making a single transliteration for Arabic, and the ISO has a transliteration standard [101], but in this case it is difficult because the initial options for input are so variable. Arabic has sounds that do not exist in Latin-based languages, and the ways of displaying them are highly varied. A speaker may be able to understand the meaning phonetically [102], but a computer machine cannot easily translate them back and forth. There is also the issue of dialects of Arabic—recently, an Egyptian friend scoffed and told me that the Algerians do not speak real Arabic. To this, an Algerian friend responded that it is the Egyptians who did not know how to speak!

Deciphering names, determining how to best format them, and building databases of those names and their variations are increasingly important in our ever more digital world. Author disambiguation for authors of papers in scientific journals is a recent popular area since the introduction of author networks such as the American Institute of Physics' former UniPHY platform and the Elsevier SciVal [103] (formerly Collexis [104]) platform. The common examples are for Asian names because they can be so easily inverted—putting the family name first and the given name last—by those who do not know the syntax and naming conventions and are easily confused by them. There are many Asian authors in Western journals. Trying to distinguish the names written in languages like Arabic, Tamil, and other alphabetic scripts that do not conform to the Western notion of naming conventions precludes simple solutions to complex options for names. In addition, names change as people marry, divorce, use nicknames, use or don't use middle names, and use or don't use initials.

We believe that the need for transliteration standards, like the large number of them available from ISO, and the accompanying tools and authority file databases of names, will continue to become more important as we try to bridge the divides of information capture and sharing. Unicode can be used to ensure that all character sets can be represented. Entity (people, places, and things) extraction tools need to pull as much conceptual value from the digital objects as available. Making sure that the desired information can be extracted in any language and then gathered with the aliases of each name is essential for an effective name disambiguation framework.

4.5   DATA VISUALIZATION AND TEXT ANALYTICS

Data visualization [105] and text analytics [106] are closely related to each other.

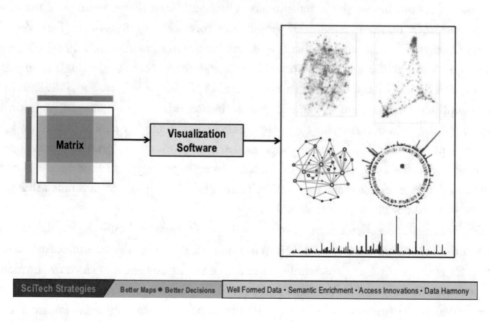

Figure 4.22: Strategies for visualizing data, with several output display options shown in the box on the right. Kevin Boyack of SciTech Strategies created this as part of his presentation at the 2014 DHUG meeting.

Text analytics is a popular topic, and becoming more so. It can be done in many different ways. Our focus here is how to do it by leveraging taxonomies. Usually, large full text files are run through a considerable amount of Bayesian, neural net, and latent semantic indexing, and other kinds of statistical-processing algorithms and engines to figure out how to compare concepts. You could do that using a taxonomy instead, and still figure out the strengths of the organization—

what are the strengths in the publications and what are the emerging topics in your research areas, to give a couple of examples. Using your own data to address these questions and figure out the answers can be beneficial for figuring out trends in research areas or coming up with an idea for a new journal title.

This area is not to be confused with text mining, the process of pulling concepts or people, places, and things out of text. A similar set of techniques is used in text mining, but the effect and use are quite different. Techniques include word frequency distributions, lexical analysis, co-occurrence, pattern recognition, link analysis, visualization, predictive analytics, and the general natural language processing (NLP) methods.

4.5.1   IEEE CASE STUDY

In this particular case, we gathered ten years of content from the National Institutes of Health's PubMed [107] database, ten years of publications from the Institute of Electrical and Electronics Engineers (IEEE) [108] publications, and ten years of the data from the United States Patent and Trademark Office [109]. We auto indexed all of the content using the Medical Subject Headings (MeSH) [110], the IEEE thesaurus, and the Defense Technical Information Center (DTIC) [111] thesaurus. This provided nine different sets of tagged data. Then we compared them to see:

Where is the field going?

What is the next event?

What are the trends?

Where are the edges of the fields?

We were able to do divide the data into sections by each year, and we mapped the terms to show the distributions and figure out where the overlaps were in research areas, where things were pulling apart, groups that have changed or augmented what they do, and ones that could be enlarged or generally marketed to. We found answers to questions like:

What are the new trends in the business?

What are the new pieces of information that the institute needs to deal with?

The product was a set of 408 images showing many different ways to display the same sets of data, each showing different trends and connections. We used exactly the same data from that nine-point matrix and displayed it in a number of different visual applications—and they surfaced very different information. The examples in the figure above show some of the possible views. The long line graph at the bottom, when wrapped around in a circle, shows the same data in a different way. In this matrix view, we have blue and red areas—red represents medical literature and blue represents engineering content—and where they overlap is the field of bioengineering. This methodology is good for showing business intelligence and data mining organizations how to harness the concepts from the taxonomy tagged to the actual data to show the real trends using a content and data foundation for the projections.

4.6   NEW PLATFORMS

A taxonomy supports delivery of content in a very precise way, providing exactly what the user wants. Using a mobile device, you usually don't have the time to sort through a million hits from Google. The user wants very precise answers with very good recall so that they are retrieving what they need, but only the results that are precisely on topic. Relevance in mobile applications is a bit of a canard [112] because it is just a guess—a confidence factor in the search results. As your user, I don't really want your estimate of confidence that you are answering my question correctly. I want you to absolutely answer my question precisely when, for example, I am looking for a gas station while on a road trip because my car is running on fumes. Although the rates for connection time seem to be getting lower with more all-inclusive and unlimited options from mobile providers, the screens of mobile devices are still necessarily smaller than those for our desktop or laptop computers. Seeing a million possible hits for a given search displayed on my mobile device would be overwhelming and not very useful.

4.6.1   TAXONOMIES IN E-COMMERCE

E-commerce is another way to use taxonomies, and we discussed this a little in the preceding chapter. Amazon [113], L.L.Bean [114], and eBay [115] are examples of some e-commerce sites that use taxonomies to their advantage. Take a look at the Amazon site, under the "Shop by Department" drop-down menu. The categorizations there are the top terms in their taxonomy. When you click on one of those categories, or top terms, it then displays more detail, which is the second level of the taxonomy. We can click on "Books and Audible," and then we see a list with "Books," "Kindle Books," "Children's Books," "Textbooks," and "Magazines." When I click on "Children's Books", I then see the third level of their taxonomy, which includes "Baby-Age 2," "Ages 3–5," "Ages 6–8," Ages 9–12," and "Shop All." As I click on each successive lower level, or narrower category, I get closer to the items that will be acceptable within my parameters. After three clicks, the site displays individual titles and I can select from those. Remember, as we discussed in previous chapter(s), that our web users generally don't want to go any more than three levels or three clicks deep. The concept for web searching is three clicks—any more than that and the users have lost interest.

Figure 4.23: Amazon.com Children's Books category, August 18, 2014.

To complicate this slightly, however, on the left side of the page, there are options "Shop by Category," "Featured in Children's Books," and "Featured Formats." Below that, also on the left, are places where I can shop by facet—"Age Range," "Leveling Standards," "New Releases," "Department," "Format," "Language," "Eligible for Free Shipping," "Award Winners," "Promotion," "Avg. Customer Review," "International Shipping," "Condition," and "Availability" (next to each item within each category, there is a number in parentheses. That number indicates how many titles are listed in their database that fit within that subcategory). I can choose attributes from any one or all of these options, and each time I do that, it refines my search until there are a discrete number of results that fit my parameters. As I click on those and narrow my search, though, the rest of the page starts to display individual titles. The displayed titles match my attribute selections, so in this instance I continue clicking to cull the options down to a manageable size selection on which I can make my purchase decision.

Amazon also uses their taxonomy for suggestive selling [116]. In my example above, I clicked on the title *The Lost Hero,* by Rick Riordan—a favorite author of my granddaughter. At the bottom of the page, two new areas appear—one titled "Frequently Bought Together" that shows my selected title and two other titles by Rick Riordan, along with a handy total dollar amount for the bundle, and one titled "Customers Who Bought This Item Also Bought," which displays even more additional titles by the same author, as well as many additional titles by several other authors. When e-commerce site operators use this approach, they usually report increased sales overall—and they did this using their taxonomy, suggesting books that had some taxonomy terms in common with the book that I chose and not just the author's name.

4.6.2   TAXONOMY RECOMMENDATION ENGINE

You can accomplish the same thing in your organization by using the taxonomy as a recommendation engine. When additional items in the database are tagged with the same terms or terms as one selected by the user, then those additional items are likely to be of interest to the searcher. Your interface can tell users, "People who clicked on this article may also be interested in this one...," and then list bibliographic citations of articles with similar subject or semantic profiles. This will encourage them to stay on your site and search for more. The search will link and serve "more like these" based on what the user was searching for.

Here we have talked about many of the ways that a taxonomy can be leveraged in a search system or on a website that is backed by a search system. Some of these options are interesting to play with but may not yet be applied in a way that generates revenue, and others clearly are. Human ingenuity will continue, I hope, to dream up other novel and innovative ways to use well-formed data—and taxonomic resources—to great advantage. I wonder what will happen years from now, when my granddaughter is an adult and wants to find a new book to read or buy clothing, or when she is in college and writing a research paper. What kinds of options will be available to her?

CHAPTER 5

What Lies Ahead for Knowledge Organization?

5.1 LOOKING THROUGH A CRYSTAL BALL

The future is always hard to predict, but very interesting to think about. I am often asked what I think the future holds for information science, knowledge organization, controlled vocabularies, search, and all kinds of other related topics. I won't pretend to be clairvoyant, but with my experience "in the trenches" on client projects, professional society involvement, committee participation, and other activities, I can make some educated guesses. Here are a few comments about what I see coming down the road.

1. More organizations will be building and implementing taxonomies. The awareness of controlled vocabularies and their applications continues to grow. They will be applied not just in publishing but in websites, association offerings, commerce online, and records management and retention. There are many ways to leverage a taxonomy, and information architects have only brushed the surface in their applications.

2. Medical organizations will also embrace alternatives to number-based classification systems such as ICD-9 and ICD-10, and to the complexity of government-driven coding to find accuracy through taxonomic means.

3. Taxonomies, controlled vocabularies, interoperability, and linked data will become mainstream for corporations. Publishers and associations will also actively embrace the needs for control over ever-growing collections. Universities and government will be late adopters, despite the federal government's early initiative pushing better information access.

4. It is true that vocabulary control has been around for well over 100 years, so many people do have backgrounds in the area and are looking for a new field to apply their skill sets. Though not difficult to learn, it is best learned and mastered through practice. The standards outline the options and there are many webinars, reading materials, and other training opportunities available. With the increase in taxonomies, there is also an explosion of "carpet baggers"—people who see a hot trend and

are leaping on the bandwagon with newly heralded expertise. Buyers of taxonomy services should thoroughly check credentials and expertise.

5. The Dublin Core (DC) will be reborn. I know it has been around for a long time—I have a few scars to show for it myself. But when the standard for the syntax of digital object identifiers (Z39.84) was "passed," it was by inventing a new way to get around the standards consensus requirement, using a new program called "fast tracking." Now, 15 years later, the reasons it got seven "NO" votes have not changed. Why the no votes? Dublin Core did not provide a consistent set of labels and a measurable standard, but rather is a guideline with suggested fields. It is now getting an implementation-related appraisal and serious consideration on what the functional requirements need to be and how to make DC work as a real measurable standard rather than a guideline. The new crop of DC advocates will make it happen. In addition, the advocates for linked data and those involved with the DC are working together to bring real change and education to the broader community of potential implementers.

6. The ontology name is so cool and trendy. Not many who use the word are really sure what it means, and very few mean a vocabulary structured according to the Web Ontology Language, supported by the W3C OWL standard http://www.w3.org, when they use it. Having said that, I think we will all be talking more about ontologies and less about taxonomies (and certainly not thesauri) this year. We might still mean the same thing, but our words to describe it will change. Within our own business there was the transition from "thesaurus" to "taxonomy" when CMS software with modules became prevalent.

7. We will need to figure out how to bridge the gap between professional indexing and folksonomic social tagging, while maintaining accuracy and authority.

8. I don't think the World Wide Semantic Web as originally envisioned by Tim Berners-Lee will happen soon. In fact, I don't think it will ever happen as it was originally envisioned. It is just too complicated, and so far no search system to support it for large data sets has gotten out of the lab. Just as SGML gave way to HTML and then XML, the semantic web will fade and linked data will rise.

9. I do think that the linked data initiatives will take the lead. I expect that the linked data community will move past its focus on syntax and start talking about implementation and application. They will lead the way by showing the many ways it can be done. There is no single path needed to make those links. Mashups using linked data will become much more common. Some of these mashups are already very ac-

tive sites, like the presentations done by the Cornell Ornithology laboratory for bird migrations. Many more will follow.

10. Big data lends itself very well to organization and filtering using taxonomies. Even within large undifferentiated collections—like records management archives. It is possible to use the taxonomy to provide a categorization filter for which items need to be kept and which can be discarded, working via the appropriate retention rules.

11. Interoperability of data will increase with consistent standards and tagging of the data using an organization-wide taxonomy.

5.2 ONTOLOGY AND SEMANTIC NETWORK IMPLEMENTATION: NOT FOR EVERYONE YET, BUT YOU CAN PREPARE FOR IT NOW

As knowledge organization systems increase in complexity, we have increasing numbers of dimensions, features, and ways to define the terms. Semantic networks help with bringing all those concepts together and tagging them so that you can look at them in a multitude of different ways. Currently the direction with most activity and promise is the implementation of taxonomies in triple stores using linked data protocols as discussed earlier in the book. Ontological search at the moment is done using triples.

The concepts are still the nodes. The nodes represent articles, paragraphs, and other information objects on those topics. What we are trying to do is to connect that information to our information. We need to connect conceptual treatment to the document. That is the way you can surface the conceptual nodes, represented by the taxonomy terms, search or display them, or browse, or offer a collection on a topic.

Many different systems are in use. There is much talk of semantic networks and achievement of them is only beginning. Everybody wants to have a semantic web, a semantic leverage. To me, the work based on Tim Berners-Lee's conception of the semantic web [117] has become so over-engineered that it will never be successful. But the concepts at the base of it all are really intriguing and I think will be implemented by the simpler linked data movement, just as SGML was replaced by XML. The movement is toward the implementation of triple stores based on taxonomies' relationships to the actual content. The triples can be used to link out to other resources throughout the web from definitions to specific sites, providing a rich search experience for the user. They are wonderful for commerce applications, like the ordering of parts or hardware.

Current discussions about ontologies and a semantic network are really describing an ideal that has not yet been achieved. I think we ought to be ready to embrace ontologies and semantic webs when and where it is feasible. Right now it is beginning to be truly feasible using triple set and linked data protocols. As I write there are three organizations that can support serious sized collections: The Stationary Office (TSO), the MarkLogic Corporation, and Publishing Technologies. All three have installations with over a million triples in their triple stores using taxonomic approaches for the concept linking. A full ontology is still a great many links, expensive to build, and it is difficult to find a search system to implement it on content once you have the ontology and the data tagged. If you have 600,000 or 1.2 million documents, you should build a taxonomy, tag the records, and then add the ontology and links built on that very firm foundation. That way you can move quickly to a new platform when it is available and still leverage rich semantic data now.

There are some prototypes and early implementers as I just described. The information scientist in the lab can create a perfect 5,000-document, functional semantic model. But is it scalable to larger collections? When he adds the 5,001st document, does it crash? Generally the data sets are small for the prototypes, and the papers written to describe the technology are published in *Transactions of the ACM* (Association for Computing Machinery [118]) or the *Journal of ASIS&T* [119]. Some of the papers I have seen only use a document collection of 7 or 50 documents., not large enough to draw scalable and commercial implementations. If you have a collection of more than 5,000 objects, I suggest you tag it with a taxonomy and then you are in an excellent position to get yourself something that could become a semantic network. When someone figures out a way to implement it, you'll be all set to go. You can work toward that goal now. Tag your data well, get a controlled vocabulary implemented, and keep improving on the term base you have. With those building blocks, and applying the term tags to your content, you will be well positioned to move forward.

Tag your data now. Build your thesaurus or taxonomy now. These activities will serve you well as the future of information and knowledge management becomes the here and now.

Glossary

AACR, AACR2

See Anglo-American Cataloguing Rules.

Accuracy (in search results)

The quality of search results, as measured by any of a variety of metrics or determined by subjective factors.

All-and-some rule, All-and-some test

A method for evaluating the validity of broader term–narrower term relationships. *Some* of whatever a broader term represents should be represented by each of its narrower terms, and *all* of what a narrower term represents should fit within the concept represented by a broader term.

Amarakosha (also _Namalinganushasana_)

An ancient Indian thesaurus written in Sanskrit. It reportedly served as an inspiration for *Roget's Thesaurus*.

American National Standards Institute (ANSI)

The official standards organization for the United States.

Anglo-American Cataloguing Rules (AACR, AACR2)

A set of guidelines (or the publication containing those guidelines) used by library catalogers as their style guide. It has been published jointly by the American Library Association, the Canadian Library Association, and the U.K.'s Chartered Institute of Library and Information Professionals. In 2010, AACR2 (the 2nd edition of AACR) was succeeded by the Resource Description and Access (RDA) cataloging standard.

ANSI/NISO Z39.19 (Z39.19)

An American National Standard developed by the National Information Standards Organization (NISO), and approved July 25, 2005, by the American National Standards Institute (ANSI). Establishes a basic vocabulary for the theory and application of terminology work. It was reaffirmed in 2010 without revision as ANSI/NISO Z39.19-2005 (R2010), and is known by a variety of designations similar to that one. The full title is *Guidelines for the Construction, Format, and Management of Monolingual Controlled Vocabularies*. The 2010 version is referred to in this book as Z39.19-2010R.

Ant colony optimization (ACO)

> An algorithmic approach to task optimization based on the behavior of ants. The probability that an ant will choose a particular path is proportional to the number of times that other ants have already chosen that path, creating a positive feedback loop. ACO algorithms are being developed and researched for a wide variety of task optimization problems, including data classification.

API (Application programming interface)

> Programming code that a computer system provides for supporting requests made of that system by a computer program. Often used to refer to the software that implements an API.

Associative relationship

> As defined in ANSI/NISO Z39.19-2010R, "*A relationship between or among terms in a controlled vocabulary that leads from one term to other terms that are related to or associated with it.*" A pair of terms that have an associative relationship is known as related terms; this relationship is often indicated by the acronym "RT."

Author submission system, Submission management system

> An online platform on which authors can submit articles and associated information directly to a publisher (usually of an online article database). Often, this same platform can also be used by the editorial staff to manage peer review, internal and author review of the draft and proposed changes, and other workflow aspects of the publication process.

Authority file, Authority list

> As defined in ANSI/NISO Z39.19-2010R, "*A set of established headings and the cross-references to be made to and from each heading, often citing the authority for the preferred form or variants. Types of authority files include name authority files and subject authority files.*"

Auto-categorization, Auto-indexing

> Computer-automated subject indexing.

Auto-completion

> In search interfaces, a feature that produces a display of possible search words or phrases, sometimes based on an associated taxonomy or thesaurus, when a user starts typing a search string. In Google and similar search platforms, the completion is based on previous queries.

Bayes' theorem

> A major statistical principle, involving the calculation of probability based on prior statistical evidence.

Bayesian search

> In information retrieval, the use of probability calculation methods based on Bayes' theorem to determine the likelihood of potential information resources being relevant to specific searches.

Binomial nomenclature (Binominal nomenclature, Binary nomenclature)

The standard system used by biologists for designating biological organisms with two-word Latin or pseudo-Latin names. The first word indicates the genus to which an organism is assumed to belong, and the second word indicates the appropriate species name within that genus.

Boolean algebra, Boolean logic

A form of algebra in which logical expressions contain one or more Boolean operators (AND, OR, NOT) to define sets.

Boolean search

A type of information search that uses the operators of Boolean logic (AND, OR, NOT), in combination with two or more search strings, to filter search results.

Bottom-up approach (in controlled vocabulary construction)

As explained in ANSI/NISO Z39.19-2010R, "*the necessary hierarchical structures and relationships are created as the work proceeds, but starting from the terms having the narrowest scope and moving to the more generic ones.*"

British Standards Institution, BSI (aka BSI Group)

The organization officially recognized by the government of the United Kingdom as the U.K.'s National Standards Body. BSI is the U.K. member of the international standards organizations, ISO and IEC.

Broader term

As defined in ANSI/NISO Z39.19-2010R, "*A term to which another term or multiple terms are subordinate in a hierarchy. In thesauri, the relationship indicator for this type of term is BT.*"

Browsing

As defined in ANSI/NISO Z39.19-2010R, "*The process of visually scanning through organized collections of representations of content objects, controlled vocabulary terms, hierarchies, taxonomies, thesauri, etc.*"

Candidate term

As defined in ANSI/NISO Z39.19-2010R, "*A term under consideration for admission into a controlled vocabulary because of its potential usefulness.*"

Classification scheme

As defined in ANSI/NISO Z39.19-2010R, "*A method of organization according to a set of pre-established principles, usually characterized by a notation system and a hierarchical structure of relationships among the entities.*"

Collabulary

As defined by Jonathon Keats, "*A collaborative vocabulary for tagging Web content. Like the folksonomies used on social bookmarking sites like del.icio.us [now Delicious], collabularies are generated by a community. But unlike folksonomies, they're automatically vetted for consistency, extracting the wisdom of crowds from the cacophony.*" (Jonathon Keats, "Jargon Watch," *Wired*, January 1, 2007)

Colon classification

A library classification system developed by S.R. Ranganathan. It is reputed to be the first faceted classification system.

Compound term

As defined in ANSI/NISO Z39.19-2010R, "*A term consisting of more than one word that represents a single concept.*"

Controlled vocabulary

As defined in ANSI/NISO Z39.19-2010R:

"*A list of terms that have been enumerated explicitly. This list is controlled by and is available from a controlled vocabulary registration authority. All terms in a controlled vocabulary must have an un-ambiguous, non-redundant definition.* **NOTE**: *This is a design goal that may not be true in practice; it depends on how strict the controlled vocabulary registration authority is regarding registration of terms into a controlled vocabulary.*

"*At a minimum, the following two rules must be enforced:*

"*1. If the same term is commonly used to mean different concepts, then its name is explicitly qualified to resolve this ambiguity.* **NOTE**: *This rule does not apply to synonym rings.*

"*2. If multiple terms are used to mean the same thing, one of the terms is identified as the preferred term in the controlled vocabulary and the other terms are listed as synonyms or aliases.*"

"Registration authority" refers to any taxonomy editor or taxonomy team that has some sort of authorization for control of the vocabulary. Alternatively, the organization granting them the authority will serve the purpose.

COSATI

The Federal Council on Science and Technology's Committee on Scientific and Technical Information. It was operational from the early 1960s to the early 1970s.

Cutter Expansive Classification (often referred to as **Cutter classification**)

A library classification system developed by Charles Ammi Cutter in the 1880s. It serves as the basis for the Library of Congress Classification.

Data visualization

The use of a graphical visual representation to convey or interpret data.

DCMI

See Dublin Core Metadata Initiative.

Descriptor

See Preferred term.

Dewey Decimal Classification (commonly known as the **Dewey Decimal System)**

A library classification system developed by Melvil Dewey in the 1870s and 1880s. It formed the basis of the Universal Decimal Classification.

Dublin Core, Dublin Core Metadata Element Set

As described by the Dublin Core Metadata Initiative at http://dublincore.org/documents/dces/, "*The Dublin Core Metadata Element Set is a vocabulary of fifteen properties for use in resource description. The name 'Dublin' is due to its origin at a 1995 invitational workshop in Dublin, Ohio; 'core' because its elements are broad and generic, usable for describing a wide range of resources.*" This core metadata element set is usually referred to as "Dublin Core."

Dublin Core Metadata Initiative (DCMI)

According to DCMI's website (http://dublincore.org/), "*The Dublin Core Metadata Initiative, or 'DCMI,' is an open organization supporting innovation in metadata design and best practices across the metadata ecology. DCMI's activities include work on architecture and modeling, discussions and collaborative work in DCMI Communities and DCMI Task Groups, global conferences, meetings and workshops, and educational efforts to promote widespread acceptance of metadata standards and best practices.*" DCMI is the main promulgator of the Dublin Core metadata standards.

Editorial note

A note connected with a controlled vocabulary term (usually in a designated field in the term record), for the purpose of communicating information having to do with in-house editorial and vocabulary development matters. Editorial notes are generally not exposed to Internet display.

Enterprise software

Software designed for use by several people simultaneously within an organization.

Entry term, Non-preferred term

A synonym or quasi-synonym for a preferred term. Non-preferred terms are not used for indexing, but can direct a manual indexer or an automated indexing system to use the corresponding preferred terms. "Entry terms" (but not "non-preferred terms") may also be considered to include indexing terms.

Epistemology, Theory of knowledge

The philosophical field covering the study of the nature of knowledge.

Equivalence relationship

As defined in ANSI/NISO Z39.19-2010R, *"A relationship between or among terms in a controlled vocabulary that leads to one or more terms that are to be used instead of the term from which the cross-reference is made."*

Faceted classification, Faceted taxonomy

A method of taxonomic classification in which terms or subjects are placed in a variety of mutually exclusive categories (such as color or location), in order to reflect various aspects or dimensions of each subject.

Faceted search, Fielded search

Search of information organized or indexed according to a faceted classification system, allowing multiple filters for narrowing of the search according to variety of dimensions or aspects. Often used in e-commerce.

Hierarchical relationship

As defined in ANSI/NISO Z39.19-2010R, *"A relationship between or among terms in a controlled vocabulary that depicts broader (generic) to narrower (specific) or whole–part relationships; begins with the words broader term (BT), or narrower term (NT)."*

Hierarchy

As defined in ANSI/NISO Z39.19-2010R, *"Broader (generic) to narrower (specific) or whole–part relationships, which are generally indicated in a controlled vocabulary through codes or indentation."*

Homograph

As defined in ANSI/NISO Z39.19-2010R: *"One of two or more words that have the same spelling, but different meanings and origins. In controlled vocabularies, homographs are generally distinguished by qualifiers."* I discourage the use of qualifiers, and encourage the use of other means whenever possible to differentiate homograms (homographs).

Indexing

As defined in ANSI/NISO Z39.19-2010R, *"A method by which terms or subject headings from a controlled vocabulary are selected by a human or computer to represent the concepts in or attributes of a content object. The terms may or may not occur in the content object."* This kind of indexing should not be confused with indexing processes for creating a book index or a data index.

Indexing term

As defined in ANSI/NISO Z39.19-2010R, *"The representation of a concept in an indexing language, generally in the form of a noun or noun phrase. Terms, subject headings, and heading-sub-heading combinations are examples of indexing terms. Also called descriptor."*

Keyword

> As defined in ANSI/NISO Z39.19-2010R, *"A word occurring in the natural language of a document that is considered significant for indexing and retrieval."* Keywords can be assigned to a work by its author(s), or can be words used in search queries.

LCSH

> See *Library of Congress Subject Headings.*

Library of Congress Classification

> The system of library classification developed and maintained by the Library of Congress. It is used by many university and research libraries, as well as by the Library of Congress, for classifying library holdings.

Library of Congress Subject Headings (LCSH)

> A thesaurus of subject headings maintained and used by the Library of Congress for subject metadata in library catalog records.

Linked data

> Structured data that is connected with other data resources, based on some relationships considered to be useful, with each piece of data identified by an http URI.

Literary warrant (See also User warrant, Organizational warrant)

> As defined in ANSI/NISO Z39.19-2010R, *"Justification for the representation of a concept in an indexing language or for the selection of a preferred term because of its frequent occurrence in the literature."*

MARC (Machine-Readable Cataloging)

> A set of digital formats for the bibliographic description of library holdings, developed by the Library of Congress and now an international standard.

Machine-assisted indexing

> Indexing using software that suggests indexing terms from one or more controlled vocabularies, but that allows a human indexer to make the final determination as to which terms will be used for indexing of each resource.

MeSH (Medical Subject Headings)

> A thesaurus of subject headings developed and maintained by the U.S. National Library of Medicine (NLM), and used by NLM for cataloging MEDLINE and PubMed articles.

Metadata

> There are many kinds of metadata. Metadata is data about data—it provides the overview of an item. This book mostly refers to subject metadata from a thesaurus but descriptive metadata is the most common usage. Descriptive metadata is used to provide descriptive information about information resources. In bibliographic records and similar metadata re-

cords, the terms for the subject metadata record fields are typically obtained from a taxonomy, thesaurus, or similar classification scheme. In addition to subject and descriptive metadata, records can contain structural metadata and administrative metadata.

Narrower term

As defined in ANSI/NISO Z39.19-2010R, "*A term that is subordinate to another term or to multiple terms in a hierarchy. In thesauri, the relationship indicator for this type of term is NT.*"

National Information Standards Organization (NISO)

As NISO describes itself at http://www.niso.org/about/, "*NISO, the National Information Standards Organization, a non-profit association accredited by the American National Standards Institute (ANSI), identifies, develops, maintains, and publishes technical standards to manage information in our changing and ever-more digital environment. NISO standards apply both traditional and new technologies to the full range of information-related needs, including retrieval, re-purposing, storage, metadata, and preservation.*"

Natural language

As defined in ANSI/NISO Z39.19-2010R, "*A language used by human beings for verbal communication. Words extracted from natural language texts for indexing purposes without vocabulary control are often called keywords.*"

Natural language processing (NLP)

Computer processing of text presented in natural language.

Navigation (See also **Browsing)**

As defined in ANSI/NISO Z39.19-2010R, "*The process of moving through a controlled vocabulary or an information space via some pre-established links or relationships. For example, navigation in a controlled vocabulary could mean moving from a broader term to one or more narrower terms using the predefined relationships.*"

NISO, National Information Standards Organization

As NISO describes itself at http://www.niso.org/about/, "*NISO, the National Information Standards Organization, a non-profit association accredited by the American National Standards Institute (ANSI), identifies, develops, maintains, and publishes technical standards to manage information in our changing and ever-more digital environment. NISO standards apply both traditional and new technologies to the full range of information-related needs, including retrieval, re-purposing, storage, metadata, and preservation.*"

NLP

See *Natural language processing.*

Node label

As defined in ANSI/NISO Z39.19-2010R, "*A 'dummy' term, often a phrase, that is not assigned to documents when indexing, but which is inserted into the hierarchical section of some controlled vocabularies to indicate the logical basis on which a class has been divided. Node labels may also be used to group categories of related terms in the alphabetic section of a controlled vocabulary."*

Non-preferred term, Entry term

A synonym or quasi-synonym for a preferred term. Non-preferred terms are not used for indexing, but can direct a manual indexer or an automated indexing system to use the corresponding preferred terms. "Entry terms" (but not "non-preferred terms") may also be considered to include indexing terms.

ONIX (Online Information eXchange)

As described by EDitEUR, one of several organizations involved in the development of ONIX, *"an XML-based family of international standards intended to support computer-to-computer communication between parties involved in creating, distributing, licensing or otherwise making available intellectual property in published form, whether physical or digital."*

Ontology

As explained by the World Wide Web Consortium (W3C) at http://www.w3.org/standards/semanticweb/ontology, *"There is no clear division between what is referred to as 'vocabularies' and 'ontologies.' The trend is to use the word 'ontology' for more complex, and possibly quite formal collection of terms, whereas 'vocabulary' is used when such strict formalism is not necessarily used or only in a very loose sense."*

Organizational warrant (See also **User warrant, Literary warrant)**

As defined in ANSI/NISO Z39.19-2010R, *"Justification for the representation of a concept in an indexing language or for the selection of a preferred term due to characteristics and context of the organization."*

OWL (Web Ontology Language)

An XML-based format designed by the World Wide Web Consortium (W3C) for use in ontologies. As described by W3C at http://www.w3.org/standards/techs/owl#w3c_all, *"The OWL Web Ontology Language is designed for use by applications that need to process the content of information instead of just presenting information to humans. OWL facilitates greater machine interpretability of Web content than that supported by XML, RDF, and RDF Schema (RDF-S) by providing additional vocabulary along with a formal semantics. OWL has three increasingly-expressive sublanguages: OWL Lite, OWL DL, and OWL Full."*

Permuted display

As defined in Z39.19, *"A type of index where individual words of a term are rotated to bring each word of the term into alphabetical order in the term list."*

Polyhierarchy

The property of a taxonomy or thesaurus whereby a term can exist in more than one place in the overall hierarchical structure, having multiple broader terms.

Post-coordination

> As defined in ANSI/NISO Z39.19-2010R, "*The combining of terms at the searching stage rather than at the subject heading list construction stage or indexing stage.*"

Pre-coordination

> As defined in ANSI/NISO Z39.19-2010R, "*The formulation of a multiword heading or the linking of a heading and subheadings to create a formally controlled, multi-element expression of a concept or object.*"

Precision (in search results)

> As defined in ANSI/NISO Z39.19-2010R, "*A measure of a search system's ability to retrieve only relevant content objects. Usually expressed as a percentage calculated by dividing the number of retrieved relevant content objects by the total number of content objects retrieved.*"

Preferred term

> As defined in ANSI/NISO Z39.19-2010R, "*One of two or more synonyms or lexical variants selected as a term for inclusion in a controlled vocabulary.*"

Provisional term

> See *Candidate term.*

RDA (Resource Description and Access)

> A set of guidelines published jointly in 2010 by the American Library Association, the Canadian Library Association, and the U.K.'s Chartered Institute of Library and Information Professionals, and intended to replace the *Anglo-American Cataloguing Rules*, 2nd Edition (AACR2).

RDF (Resource Description Framework)

> As described by the World Wide Web Consortium (W3C) at http://www.w3.org/RDF/, "*RDF is a standard model for data interchange on the Web. RDF has features that facilitate data merging even if the underlying schemas differ, and it specifically supports the evolution of schemas over time without requiring all the data consumers to be changed. RDF extends the linking structure of the Web to use URIs to name the relationship between things as well as the two ends of the link (this is usually referred to as a 'triple'). Using this simple model, it allows structured and semi-structured data to be mixed, exposed, and shared across different applications.*"

Recall (in search results)

> As defined in ANSI/NISO Z39.19, "*A measure of a search system's ability to retrieve all relevant content objects. Usually expressed as a percentage calculated by dividing the number of retrieved relevant content objects by the number of all relevant content objects in a collection.*"

Reciprocity (of term relationships)

> As explained in ANSI/NISO Z39.19, "*Semantic relationships in controlled vocabularies must be reciprocal, that is each relationship from one term to another must also be represented by a recip-*

rocal relationship in the other direction. Reciprocal relationships may be symmetric, e.g. RT / RT, or asymmetric e.g., BT/NT."

Related term

As defined in ANSI/NISO Z39.19, *"A term that is associatively but not hierarchically linked to another term in a controlled vocabulary."* It is intended to expand the searcher's awareness of the vocabulary, suggesting other concepts that may be of interest.

Resource Description and Access

See RDA.

Scope note

As defined in ANSI/NISO Z39.19-2010R, *"A note following a term explaining its coverage, specialized usage, or rules for assigning it."*

Semantic Web

As described by the World Wide Web Consortium (W3C) at http://www.w3.org/2001/ sw/, *"The Semantic Web is about two things. It is about common formats for integration and combination of data drawn from diverse sources, where on the original Web mainly concentrated on the interchange of documents. It is also about language for recording how the data relates to real world objects. That allows a person, or a machine, to start off in one database, and then move through an unending set of databases which are connected not by wires but by being about the same thing."*

SKOS (Simple Knowledge Organization System)

According to the World Wide Web Consortium (W3C) at http://www.w3.org/TR/ skos-reference/, *"a common data model for sharing and linking knowledge organization systems via the Web. Many knowledge organization systems, such as thesauri, taxonomies, classification schemes and subject heading systems, share a similar structure, and are used in similar applications. SKOS captures much of this similarity and makes it explicit, to enable data and technology sharing across diverse applications. The SKOS data model provides a standard, low-cost migration path for porting existing knowledge organization systems to the Semantic Web. SKOS also provides a lightweight, intuitive language for developing and sharing new knowledge organization systems. It may be used on its own, or in combination with formal knowledge representation languages such as the Web Ontology language (OWL)."*

Structured data

Data in which the text of each information resource is partitioned into fields, often delimited by XML "tags" or field labels indicating the kind of metadata element contained within each field.

Subject heading

As explained in ANSI/NISO Z39.19-2010R: *"A word or phrase, or any combination of words, phrases, and modifiers used to describe the topic of a content object. Precoordination of terms for multiple and related concepts is a characteristic of subject headings that distinguishes them from controlled vocabulary terms."*

Subject matter expert (SME)

In taxonomy and thesaurus development, a person who has deep knowledge of a subject area represented in the vocabulary, and who provides advice and feedback regarding such matters as term wording, hierarchical structure, appropriate non-preferred terms, and terms or concepts to consider adding.

Synonym ring

As defined in ANSI/NISO Z39.19-2010R, *"A group of terms that are considered equivalent for the purposes of retrieval."* Terms in a synonym ring are not distinguished as preferred or non-preferred.

Taxonomy

As defined in ANSI/NISO Z39.19-2010R, *"A collection of controlled vocabulary terms organized into a hierarchical structure. Each term in a taxonomy is in one or more parent/child (broader/narrower) relationships to other terms in the taxonomy."*

Term

As defined in ANSI/NISO Z39.19-2010R, *"One or more words designating a concept."*

Terminology registry

A descriptive catalog of terminologies, usually containing taxonomies and thesauri, as well as other kinds of controlled vocabularies.

Theory of knowledge

See Epistemology.

Thesaurus (plural Thesauri or Thesauruses)

As defined in ANSI/NISO Z39.19-2010R, *"A controlled vocabulary arranged in a known order and structured so that the various relationships among terms are displayed clearly and identified by standardized relationship indicators."*

Top-down approach (in controlled vocabulary construction)

As explained in ANSI/NISO Z39.19-2010R, *"The broadest terms are identified first and then narrower terms are selected to reach the desired level of specificity. The necessary hierarchical structures and relationships are created as the work proceeds."*

Training set

A set of documents used in developing the indexing capabilities of a statistics-based indexing system.

Truncation

Shortening of a word or phrase, sometimes replacing the omitted portion with a wildcard character that can represent any and all characters. This technique is used to give more comprehensive results when creating search strings or indexing rules.

Turney's algorithm

A semantic approach to sentiment analysis. A *"simple unsupervised learning algorithm for classifying reviews as recommended (thumbs up) or not recommended (thumbs down). The classification of a review is predicted by the average semantic orientation of the phrases in the review that contain adjectives or adverbs. A phrase has a positive semantic orientation when it has good associations (e.g., 'subtle nuances') and a negative semantic orientation when it has bad associations (e.g., 'very cavalier')"* (In Peter D. Turney, "Thumbs Up or Thumbs Down? Semantic Orientation Applied to Unsupervised Classification of Reviews," *Proceedings of the 40th Annual Meeting of the Association for Computational Linguistics*, Philadelphia, July 2002: 417–424).

UID

Unique identifier. An identification number or alphanumeric code often used with taxonomy and thesaurus terms, term records, and concept records.

Unicode

As described by the Unicode Consortium, at http://www.unicode.org/standard/standard.html, *"The Unicode Standard is a character coding system designed to support the worldwide interchange, processing, and display of the written texts of the diverse languages and technical disciplines of the modern world. In addition, it supports classical and historical texts of many written languages."*

Universal Decimal Classification (UDC)

As described by the UDC Consortium at www.udcc.org, *"UDC is one of the most widely used classification schemes for all fields of knowledge. It is used in libraries, bibliographic, documentation and information services in over 130 countries around the world and is published in over 40 languages."*

Unstructured text

See *Structured text*. Unstructured text lacks such metadata labeling.

User warrant

As defined in ANSI/NISO Z39.19-2010R, *"Justification for the representation of a concept in an indexing language or for the selection of a preferred term because of frequent requests for information on the concept or free-text searches on the term by users of an information storage and retrieval system."*

Vocabulary control

As defined in ANSI/NISO Z39.19-2010R: "*The process of organizing a list of terms (a) to indicate which of two or more synonymous terms is authorized for use; (b) to distinguish between homographs; and (c) to indicate hierarchical and associative relationships among terms in the context of a controlled vocabulary or subject heading list.*"

W3C, World Wide Web Consortium

As described by W3C at http://www.w3.org/Consortium/, "*The World Wide Web Consortium (W3C) is an international community where Member organizations, a full-time staff, and the public work together to develop Web standards. Led by Web inventor Tim Berners-Lee and CEO Jeffrey Jaffe, W3C's mission is to lead the Web to its full potential.*"

Web Ontology Language (OWL)

An XML-based format designed by the World Wide Web Consortium (W3C) for use in ontologies. As described by W3C at http://www.w3.org/standards/techs/owl#w3c_all, "*The OWL Web Ontology Language is designed for use by applications that need to process the content of information instead of just presenting information to humans. OWL facilitates greater machine interpretability of Web content than that supported by XML, RDF, and RDF Schema (RDF-S) by providing additional vocabulary along with a formal semantics. OWL has three increasingly-expressive sublanguages: OWL Lite, OWL DL, and OWL Full.*"

Z39.19 (ANSI/NISO Z39.19)

Taxonomy and thesaurus standard developed by the National Information Standards Organization (NISO), and approved July 25, 2005, by the American National Standards Institute (ANSI). Establishes a basic vocabulary for the theory and application of terminology work. It was reaffirmed in 2010 without revision as ANSI/NISO Z39.19-2005 (R2010), and is known by a variety of designations similar to that one. The full title is *Guidelines for the Construction, Format, and Management of Monolingual Controlled Vocabularies.* The 2010 version is referred to in this book as Z39.19-2010R. It does not embrace the vocabulary dealing with computer applications in terminology work which was covered by withdrawn standard ISO 1087-2.

End Notes

1   Definition of PERMUTE: to change the order or arrangement of; especially: to arrange in all possible ways, http://www.merriam-webster.com/dictionary/permuted.

2   http://www.getty.edu/research/tools/vocabularies/aat/.

3   The Extensible Markup Language (XML) is a simple text-based format for representing structured information: documents, data, configuration, books, transactions, invoices, and much more. It was derived from an older standard format called SGML (ISO 8879), and designed be more suitable for web use. From http://www.w3.org/standards/xml/core.

4   SKOS is an area of work developing specifications and standards to support the use of knowledge organization systems (KOS) such as thesauri, classification schemes, subject heading systems, and taxonomies within the framework of the Semantic Web. The Zthes Profile for Z39.50 provides a set of specifications prescribing the use of Z39.50 to navigate remote thesauri. A Z39.50 server conforming to this profile can expose its thesaurus to any conforming client, enabling its use in many applications. From http://www.w3.org/2004/02/skos/intro.

5   Z39.50 is an ANSI/NISO standard protocol for information retrieval. It has been widely deployed in libraries, and has also found applications in areas as diverse as geospatial searching, cultural heritage, and searching databases of complex chemical compounds. From http://zthes.z3950.org/z3950/index.html.

6   Jean Aitchison, David Bawden, and Alan Gilchrist. *Thesaurus Construction and Use: A Practical Manual*. 4th edition (Routledge, 2000) 5.

7   http://en.wikipedia.org/wiki/Wrapper_%28data_mining%29.

8   http://en.wikipedia.org/wiki/Relational_model.

9   http://en.wikipedia.org/wiki/IETF.

10   http://en.wikipedia.org/wiki/Uniform_Resource_Characteristics.

11   http://www.w3.org/RDF/.

12   http://lucene.apache.org/.

13   http://www.perfectsearchcorp.com/.

14   http://en.wikipedia.org/wiki/Bayes'_theorem.

15   http://en.wikipedia.org/wiki/Neural_networks.

16   http://en.wikipedia.org/wiki/Document_clustering.

17   https://www.iqt.org/.

18   http://www.ironmountain.com/Company/Company-News/News-Categories/Press-Releases/2010/January/27.aspx.

19   http://www.digitalreasoning.com/.

20   http://www.coveo.com/en.

21   http://www.clearviewecm.com/.

22   http://www.clearforest.com/solutions.html.

23   http://xmetal.com/.

24   http://www.temis.com/home.

25   http://www.autonomy.com/.

26   Access Innovations' Data Harmony software has eight types of conditions that can be included in complex rules. There is some natural language processing underneath the system, but only the rules level can be augmented by the users. There is no training set; rules must be built. In our case, we find that about 80% of the rules are simple and 20% need to be complex. We have found that with simple rules only, we get about 60% accuracy, and with complex rules we get about 85–95% accuracy in indexing.

27   http://www.oracle.com/us/corporate/acquisitions/endeca/index.html.

28   http://www.dataharmony.com/products/index.html.

29   http://www.teragram.com/.

30   http://www.smartlogic.com/.

31   http://www.3ds.com/products-services/exalead/.

32   http://www.mediasleuth.com/MediaSleuthSearcher/navtree/index.jsp.

33   http://www.aacr.org/.

34   http://en.wikipedia.org/wiki/Online_public_access_catalog.

35   Susan T. Dumais, E. Cutrell, and H. Chen, "Bringing order to the web: Optimizing search by showing results in context," *Proceedings of CHI'01, Human Factors in Computing Systems*, April 2001, 277–283.

36   https://www.google.com/.

37   http://www.bing.com/.

38   http://www.yahoo.com/.

39   http://www.ask.com/.

40   http://www.aol.com/.

41   http://technet.microsoft.com/en-us/library/ee781286(v=office.14).aspx.

42   http://www.google.com/enterprise/search/products/gsa.html.

43   http://aws.amazon.com/cloudsearch/.

44   http://www.autonomy.com/.

45   http://www.attivio.com/.

46   http://www.oracle.com/us/corporate/acquisitions/endeca/index.html.

47   http://www.lucidworks.com/.

48   http://www-01.ibm.com/software/data/information-optimization/.

49   http://www.sinequa.com/en/index.aspx.

50   http://www.rocketsoftware.com/products/rocket-folio-views.

51   http://lucene.apache.org/solr/.

52   http://www.elasticsearch.org/.

53   http://www.searchtechnologies.com/federated-search.html.

54   The File Traverser scans specified file directories on file servers, retrieves content of various formats, and submits it to a collection in your FAST ESP installation, http://nesfast1.scot.nhs.uk:16089/help/product_overview/concepts/c_esp_pov_Using_the_File_Traverser.html.

55   RSS stands for "Rich Site Summary" (http://en.wikipedia.org/wiki/RSS) or "Really Simple Syndication." It is a way to easily distribute a list of headlines, update notices, and sometimes content to a wide number of people. It is used by computer programs that organize those headlines and notices for easy reading, http://rss.softwaregarden.com/aboutrss.html.

56   http://en.wikipedia.org/wiki/Artificial_neural_network.

57   http://www.searchenginejournal.com/what-is-latent-semantic-indexing-seo-defined/21642/.

58   http://en.wikipedia.org/wiki/N-gram.

59   See the website of the George Boole Foundation, at http://www.boolean.org.uk/index.html.

60   http://en.wikipedia.org/wiki/Bayes%27s_theorem.

61   http://www.apperceptual.com/background.

62   http://en.wikipedia.org/wiki/Sentiment_analysis.

63   See Peter D. Turney, "Thumbs Up or Thumbs Down? Semantic Orientation Applied to Unsupervised Classification of Reviews," *Proceedings of the 40th Annual Meeting of the Association for Computational Linguistics*, Philadelphia, July 2002: 417–424.

64   http://www.hypertextbookshop.com/dataminingbook/working_version/contents/chapters/chapter001/section003/blue/page004.html.

65   http://en.wikipedia.org/wiki/Marco_Dorigo.

66   http://en.wikipedia.org/wiki/Ant_colony_optimization.

67   http://www.fnrs.be/.

68   http://code.ulb.ac.be/iridia.home.php.

69   http://www.sce.carleton.ca/netmanage/tony/swarm.html.

70   http://www.sce.carleton.ca/netmanage/tony/swarm.html.

71   "Heuristic refers to experience-based techniques for problem solving, learning, and discovery that give a solution which is not guaranteed to be optimal. Where the exhaustive search is impractical, heuristic methods are used to speed up the process of finding a satisfactory solution via mental shortcuts to ease the cognitive load of making a decision. Examples of this method include using a rule of thumb, an educated guess, an intuitive judgment, stereotyping, or common sense. In more precise terms, heuristics are strategies using readily accessible, though loosely applicable, information to control problem solving in human beings and machines," http://en.wikipedia.org/wiki/Heuristic.

72   http://en.wikipedia.org/wiki/Natural_language_processing.

73   The branch of semiotics that deals with the formal properties of signs and symbols, http://www.thefreedictionary.com/syntactics. Semiotics is the theory and study of signs and symbols, especially as elements of language or other systems of communication, and comprising semantics, syntactics, and pragmatics, http://www.thefreedictionary.com/semiotics.

74   The study or science of meaning in language; the study of relationships between signs and symbols and what they represent; or the meaning or the interpretation of a word, sentence, or other language form, http://www.thefreedictionary.com/semantics.

75   Here, refers to the study of the structure and form of words in language or a language, including inflection, derivation, and the formation of compounds, http://www.thefreedictionary.com/morphology.

76   http://nlp.stanford.edu/IR-book/html/htmledition/stemming-and-lemmatization-1.html.

77   American Society for Information Science and Technology, http://www.asis.org/.

78   http://www-users.cs.umn.edu/~kumar/dmbook/ch8.pdf.

79   http://www.digitalreasoning.com/.

80   http://en.wikipedia.org/wiki/Co-occurrence.

81   http://www.bayesian-inference.com/index.

82   http://www.searchenginejournal.com/what-is-latent-semantic-indexing-seo-defined/21642/.

83   http://en.wikipedia.org/wiki/Wildcard_character.

84   http://blog.helloreverb.com/search-vs-discovery-looking-for-the-big-idea/.

85   http://yippy.com/.

86   http://www-users.cs.umn.edu/~kumar/dmbook/dmslides/chap8_basic_cluster_analysis.pdf.

87   http://nlp.stanford.edu/IR-book/html/htmledition/hierarchical-clustering-1.html.

88   http://cgm.cs.mcgill.ca/~soss/cs644/projects/siourbas/sect5.html.

89   http://www.oracle.com/webfolder/technetwork/data-quality/edqhelp/Content/advanced_features/indexing_concept_guide.htm.

90   http://users.ics.aalto.fi/sami/thesis/node9.html.

91   http://home.deib.polimi.it/matteucc/Clustering/tutorial_html/kmeans.html.

92   http://home.deib.polimi.it/matteucc/Clustering/tutorial_html/cmeans.html.

93   https://sites.google.com/site/dataclusteringalgorithms/quality-threshold-clustering-algorithm-1.

94   http://en.wikipedia.org/wiki/Locality-sensitive_hashing.

95   http://en.wikipedia.org/wiki/Graph_theory.

96   http://en.wikipedia.org/wiki/Spectral_clustering.

97   Heather Hedden, "Faceted Search vs. Faceted Browse." The Accidental Taxonomist (blog), April 12, 2012.

98   http://www.digitalreasoning.com/.

99   http://www.spicynodes.org/.

100   http://www.xpeerient.com/.

101   http://www.iso.org/iso/iso_catalogue/catalogue_tc/catalogue_detail.htm?csnumber=2398.

102   http://en.wikipedia.org/wiki/Romanization_of_Arabic.

103   http://info.scival.com/.

104   http://www.elsevier.com/about/press-releases/science-and-technology/elsevier-acquires-collexis,-a-leading-developer-of-semantic-technology-and-knowledge-discovery-software-for-research-and-development-institutions.

105   http://visual.ly/.

106   http://en.wikipedia.org/wiki/Text_mining.

107   http://www.ncbi.nlm.nih.gov/pubmed.

108   http://www.ieee.org/index.html.

109   http://www.uspto.gov/.

110   http://www.nlm.nih.gov/mesh/.

111   http://www.dtic.mil/dtic/.

112   A false or unfounded report or story; especially a fabricated report, http://www.merriam-webster.com/dictionary/canard.

113   http://www.amazon.com/.

114   http://www.llbean.com/.

115   http://www.ebay.com/.

116   Definition of "Suggestive Selling:" A sales technique where the employee asks the customer if they would like to include an additional purchase or recommends a product which might suit the client. Suggestive selling is used to increase the purchase amount of the client and revenues of the business. Often times the additional sale is much smaller than the original purchase and is a complementary product, http://www.investopedia.com/terms/s/suggestive-selling.asp.

117   http://www.w3.org/People/Berners-Lee/.

118   http://www.acm.org/.

119   http://www.asist.org/.

Author Biography

Marjorie M.K. Hlava and her team have worked with or built over 600 controlled vocabularies. Their experience is shared with you in this book. Margie is well known internationally for her work in the implementation of information science principles and the ever-evolving technology that supports them. She and the team at Access Innovations have provided the "back room" operations for many information-related organizations over the last 40 years. Margie is very active in the main organizations concerned with those areas. She has served as president of NFAIS (the National Federation of Advanced Information Services); that organization awarded her the Anne Marie Cunningham Memorial Award for Exemplary Volunteer Service to the Federation in 2012, as well as the Miles Conrad lectureship in 2014. She has also served as president of the American Society for Information Science and Technology (ASIS&T), which has awarded her the prestigious Watson Davis Award and their top honor, the ASIS&T Award of Merit. She has served two terms on the Board of Directors of the Special Libraries Association (SLA); SLA has honored her with their President's Award for her work in standards and has made her a Fellow of the SLA for her many other services within the organization. More recently, she served as the founding chair of SLA's Taxonomy Division.

For five years, Margie was on the Board of the National Information Standards Organization (NISO), and she continues to serve on the Content and Collaboration Standards Topic Committee for NISO. She has also held numerous committee positions in these and other organizations. She convened the workshop leading to the ANSI/NISO thesaurus standard NISO Z39.19-2005, and was a member of the standards committee for its writing. She also acted as liaison to the British Standards Institute controlled vocabulary standards group to ensure that the U.S. and British standards would be compatible.

Margie is the founder and president of Access Innovations, Inc., which has been honored with many awards, including recognition several times by *KMWorld Magazine* as one of 100 Companies That Matter in Knowledge Management and as a Trend-Setting Product Company, as well as by *EContent Magazine* as one of 100 Companies That Matter Most in the Digital Content Industry. The company's information management services include thesaurus and taxonomy creation.

Under Margie's guidance, Access Innovations has developed the Data Harmony® line of software for content creation, taxonomy management, and automated categorization for portals and data collections. The Data Harmony Suite is protected by two patents, numbers 6898586 and 8046212, and 21 patent claims. Her recognition of the value of automatic code suggestion for the medical industry led to the founding of Access Integrity and its Medical Claims Compliance system.

Margie's primary areas of research include automated indexing, thesaurus development, taxonomy creation, natural language processing, machine translations, and computer aided indexing. She has authored more than 200 published articles on these subjects. At industry and association meetings, she has given numerous workshops and presentations on thesaurus and taxonomy creation and maintenance.

Printed in the United States
by Baker & Taylor Publisher Services